Channeling

Practical Techniques to Connect
With Your Spirit

*(Trust Your Intuition and Embrace the Force That
Connects Us All)*

Bryan Crary

Published By **Oliver Leish**

Bryan Crary

All Rights Reserved

Channeling: Practical Techniques to Connect With Your Spirit (Trust Your Intuition and Embrace the Force That Connects Us All)

ISBN 978-1-77485-711-3

No part of this guidebook shall be reproduced in any form without permission in writing from the publisher except in the case of brief quotations embodied in critical articles or reviews.

Legal & Disclaimer

The information contained in this ebook is not designed to replace or take the place of any form of medicine or professional medical advice. The information in this ebook has been provided for educational & entertainment purposes only.

The information contained in this book has been compiled from sources deemed reliable, and it is accurate to the best of the Author's knowledge; however, the Author cannot guarantee its accuracy and validity and cannot be held liable for any errors or omissions. Changes are periodically made to this book. You must consult your doctor or get professional medical advice before using any of the suggested remedies, techniques, or information in this book.

Upon using the information contained in this book, you agree to hold harmless the Author from and against any damages, costs, and expenses, including any legal fees potentially resulting from the application of any of the information provided by this guide. This disclaimer applies to any damages or injury caused by the use and application, whether directly or indirectly, of any advice or information presented, whether for breach of contract, tort, negligence, personal injury, criminal intent, or under any other cause of action.

You agree to accept all risks of using the information presented inside this book. You need to consult a professional medical practitioner in order to ensure you are both able and healthy enough to participate in this program.

Table Of Contents

Introduction 1

Chapter 1: Background Information About Channeling 3

Chapter 2: Core Channeling Skills 22

Chapter 3: Sharpening You Psychic Sensors 35

Chapter 4: Guide For Channeling 70

Chapter 5: Asking Right Questions 88

Chapter 6: Meeting Spirits 96

Chapter 7: Protecting Yourself 112

Chapter 8: Mediumship 126

Introduction

Channeling books may not appeal to everyone. There are many channels available and some charge for services. There are varying levels of proficiency among these individuals. Some are quite skilled and others are simply delusional. Also, there are those who pretend to be psychics and take advantage people's ignorance regarding the spirit world.

It's not easy to be a good channel, or medium. Therefore, it's a smart decision to learn channeling. You can protect yourself from the deceitful and ignorant by doing the work yourself.

Apart from that, a medium or psychic may relay messages from the spirit to your soul. However, if you don't know how to discern true contact from false, it is easy to fall for many tricks. Even if the contact appears genuine, it is best to verify the authenticity of the message before you rely on another person to act.

Spirit messages are often intimate and personal, and are meant to be transformative on many levels. You will receive more value from the message if your experience it, rather than just hearing someone say it.

This book will tell you all about channeling, how it works and what you can do to make it happen. This book will teach you a lot but you need to continue learning about the spirit realm so that you can channel more effectively. Interviewing and reading books about the spirit world is one way to do this. In order to live a more spiritual life, you need to make an effort.

Let's talk about channeling. It is a rewarding and highly rewarding practice.

Chapter 1: Background information about channeling

"Seeing death and dying as the end in life is like seeing horizons as the end in ocean."

- David Searls

Channeling is a skill anyone can learn. It's an easy skill to learn. It is worth reading this brief background to better understand the process.

What is channeling, exactly?

Channeling refers the act of retrieving information in the forms of images, sounds or words from another source. Channeling is the act of collecting the information, much like a pipe directing water. Channels are not able to create the water they hold, just as a pipe can't. The personality of a channel is only a vessel for communication.

Channeling is an ancient practice. Many religions around the globe believe that they can communicate with the spirit world. Each one has their own method.

Europe, the USA, as well as other English-speaking countries, became interested in Spiritualism. The movement centers on the belief of spirits of the dead being able to communicate with the living through mediums. There are many channels that claim to be able communicate with ancestors, angels and nature spirits. They also claim to have access to aliens, archetypes, or the Universal Mind.

How does it work?

We are unsure if channeling simply involves the mind's ability of ESP to receive information, or if there is real communication between other beings. We do know that channeling can help us gain wisdom and knowledge that goes beyond our conscious awareness.

Two things can be used to explain how channeling works: the existence spirit and the ability for people to use their psychic abilities.

Existence Of The Soul

It is believed that every thing has a spirit, which transcends death. It is believed that the soul of a person after death retains all aspects of their identity, including intelligence, personality, identity, emotions, personality, and memory. In essence, he/she will remain the same person in a new mode of existence.

These are just a few examples of evidence to support the existence of a personality even after death.

Near Death Experiences

Some people who had died and then were revived claimed to have experienced experiences that made it appear they were still alive. Many were able both to perceive the surrounding environment and other realms. Several were able to remember seeing things that they couldn't see because they weren't conscious. These people were blind, and they saw things.

Out of Body Experiences

There are people who can travel while they are still alive and move around without leaving their bodies. Some can travel to faraway lands and even appear as an apparition. OBEs can also happen unintentionally. Sometimes people even see their own bodies, and then realize that they're not there.

Reincarnation Cases

Most people forget that they have lived in the past. They may have vivid memories of having been someone else. They know their history, including where they lived in the past, with whom, what they did, and when they died. These details are sometimes verified to be true, that there really was someone who fits the descriptions that these possibly-reincarnated individuals say. Many have provided highly private information which suggests that they may be the deceased reincarnated as new bodies.

Hauntings or Visitations

A ghost might be seen if they are causing unusual phenomena such as poltergeist activities (things that move without a known cause), apparitions, strange sonic sounds and other similar signs. It is possible that other causes may exist, such as the soul or the spirit of the deceased.

For example, they might be caused or influenced by forces outside our control. But, those who have meaningful experiences with the deceased or received helpful messages from them consider these to be proof that someone lives on even after death.

Existence Multiple Dimensions

The belief system of religions or cultures is that there are other planes than the one we are most familiar. Theoretical science suggests that other dimensions exist. Math supports this possibility, but it has yet to be tested. Over time, people from all walks of life have shared their stories of seeing other worlds. The spirits may reside in these other dimensions. Unless a person becomes more attuned, it's unlikely that the average person will see them often.

There are many other things that can be considered signs that spirits exist. Even after death, the spirits of the dead are still present. To learn more about them, look up "afterlife investigation" and the "survivalof conscious".

Psychic Abilities

The ability to detect spirits and interpret their messages can be explained with psychic abilities. Parapsychologists, those who study the unexplainable abilities of the human intellect, have some theories regarding psychic abilities and how they work.

These abilities may be a result that the soul does not follow natural laws. Information can travel freely from one person or event to another without passing through sensory channels, because everything is spirit.

These are some of the more specific theories that could explain channeling, mediumship.

Electromagnetism

Early researchers believed that information travels along electromagnetic waves in a similar way to electromagnetic radiation. They claim that people are able to pick up information from thin air because they are receptive. This theory is not able to explain how psychic data can be sent faster that the speed of light or why it doesn't decrease even when sent long distances away.

Psi Dimension

Another theory says that there is another dimension above space, time, and consciousness. This dimension may intersect with the dimensions we are familiar with. Because the mind exists elsewhere, it isn't bound by laws. Therefore, people who have passed away may have gone to another dimension. In this way, the living and dead can interact using the intersections between these planes.

Quantum Connections

Quantum mechanics describes matter at the subatomic layer. In this place, they are neither waves or particles but act like either. It is also where they don't exist as "real", but only as probabilities. The rules of the quantum universe are vastly different than those of our macro-world. This includes quantum connectivity, the ability for one particle to instantly influence another particle even though they're separated by vast distances. According to quantum connection theory, consciousness can be described as quantum phenomena. Also, people can communicate with other entities via quantum encryption.

These theories are just that. They might or may not be true. More important, channeling is possible. Anyone can learn mediumship. There are many examples of spirit communications that you can find as you read more about channeling. You will channel more easily if you know more about them. Your mind will be more comfortable doing things it believes are good for you.

Channeling vs. Mediumship

While they may seem the same thing, channeling or mediumship is not always what it seems. Note that some sessions may combine both. If you don't feel comfortable using one method, don't worry.

Mediums receive information from the departed and relay it to them while on the run. They typically work with spirits who were close to their clients. Channels receive and communicate information from spirits other that the dead, including extraterrestrials (angels), discarnate entities, and angels. It is possible to channel both mediumship or channeling, depending on the type of spirit one contacts.

Channeling is the process of getting information from an individual other than the target. Mediumship is the process of acquiring information directly from the target. Mediumship typically involves a deeper state where the medium loses all sense of self. On the other hand, channeling can take place with the channel's personality intact.

This book will teach how to channel both mediumship and channeling. What you choose to do depends on your comfort and the information that you need.

Common Misconceptions

Although many people believe that spirits are able to assist the living, channeling or mediumship has only been popularized recently. According to some religions any spirit contact is considered evil, and any spirit that passes through it is a demonic being. Horror films and books that detail the horrors of communicating with spirits have exacerbated this belief. Many believe that channeling can be dangerous and should be avoided.

However, this is far from the truth. Sometimes, we gain accurate insight about things without knowing how. This could be a form channeling. Even if you don't engage in elaborate rituals and make agreements with spirit guides, this can still happen. This is a common phenomenon but some people are more affected than others.

People who argue that spirit channeling causes evil and is dangerous are exaggerating. Yes, there can be negative spirits in the spiritual world just like there can be negative people here. This doesn't mean that all spirits will cause harm.

Just like in the real world, there are protectors (police officers, bodyguards etc. There are also protectors living in the spirit realm. Your personal guardian Angel is one. You can also protect yourselves with things like shields or sigils.

Keep in mind that no spirit can harm your life if you keep control of it. You can protect yourself by cultivating a strong sense of self-control. You need to be clear about who you are, your values, and what matters most to you. It is important that you learn to be consistent in all your thoughts, words, actions, so that you have an internal strength that's not affected by conflicts.

While there will always be times when you are vulnerable, it is essential to remain resilient and stay on your feet. Even if this applies to normal situations, it will have a positive impact on your spiritual body.

Many think channeling can be silly and wasteful of time. If you don't know what to do, this is true. If you don't pay attention, you may think that you're receiving messages. However, in reality, you are just thinking about things. You could get into trouble if your actions are influenced by psychological conditions. This book will provide guidance on how to ensure you only receive real messages.

Uses for channeling

Channeling can have many benefits if done properly.

To be in open communication to the spirit world

Discover more about yourself

Information from other countries can be sent and received

Talk to departed loved one

Receive guidance from spirits - guides, masters, historical figures and others.

Spirits are a great way to make deals

Learn more about life & death

Exploring your personal consciousness

Communicating directly with the spirit realm

Rejoice in the comfort of your loved ones that have died

Provide comfort for the bereaved

To assist departed souls

Get help from angels, and other helpful beings

Get inspiration

To put an end to fear of the untimely.

To give you peace of Mind

To heal

Be entertained

Spirits may seek to communicate directly with the living.

They want them to say something.

They want to let everyone know they are OK

They want to help

They are fascinated by the living.

They want the settlement of unfinished business

They have contracts with you

These are just a few reasons to channel.

They are looking for answers

They believe that they are psychic

They are interested in learning more about unusual experiences they had and what they meant.

They are curious about everything paranormal.

They fear death, and they want to know if the afterlife exists.

They seek meaning in all things, including death.

They are eager to reach the dead and other beings.

They want to be of service to others

They are adventurous and love to seek excitement

They believe the eternal nature of the spirit.

They want to escape boredom

They want to expose mediums or psychics

They want attention.

As you can see not all reasons for channeling are sincere. It's essential to channel positive, honest thoughts if you want to make the most of channeling. You cannot hide your feelings from spirit because they are able to read people's minds. They might be more likely to avoid you if you tell them they don't mean it well. Sometimes they will just ignore you.

Quick Reminders

To channel the best, it is crucial that you have good relationships and trust with your spirit guides. Spirits can communicate with each other just like living beings. Respect spirits and channel them with care. But you don't have to take it personally.

Some people choose spiritualism simply because they don't have the ability to do anything in the "real life". Don't let that happen to you. We are sent to the physical world to learn lessons. To have a satisfying life, you don't necessarily need to become a practitioner of occultism. However, if you do decide to follow this path, it is important that you don't neglect your everyday life. If you do so, your foundation can weaken and make you more vulnerable to potential dangers.

Spirit beings want to have relationships with others, just like we do. They can also perform many functions such as counselors, protectors, healers, and so forth. They are not limited to the corporeal body, which is why they can take many forms. Just like how we can benefit form our friends, we also can benefit through their assistance.

Some of them are invisible to us. They can guide us in the right direction by influencing people or situations to be more favorable. They sometimes make themselves visible by displaying themselves, announcing who and what they are.

They usually decide how to communicate. They may refuse to respond to your request to send a message or appear in certain ways. Your job as channel is to detect subtle signals well enough to communicate them to humans.

This requires patience. If you don't possess the patience to channel, it is worth trying.

Although spirit guides assist us throughout the day, even though they are not telling us, we can make that process conscious by taking the initiative of communicating with them. They might be capable of performing many tasks for you. Be careful not to be dependent on them. Sometimes they will prefer to let go of you so that you can develop your character.

Be aware that while spirits can do many different things, they may also be bound by certain laws in the spiritual realm. It is not possible to expect them do everything we ask. Yet, they will always be able to provide something that will be beneficial to us.

You can't use spirits to make excuses for being responsible for bad behavior or for not doing what you should. Everything you do will be held responsible. They might be able to point you in the right direction but they are not able to walk that path for you. It is crucial that you clearly define your goals, values, and beliefs. This will help you to keep your mind open to the ideas of others.

You are in control of the channeling session. If the spirit behaves in ways you don't like, then dismiss them. It's not necessary to endure it. You have to conserve your energy in order for productive communication.

If you are responsible and use your common sense, you will not be in serious danger. Possession cases, which are very rare, are not caused by spirits contacting you. They are often accompanied other things, such as illness and abuse. These conditions may make possession less difficult but not necessarily lead to it. If the possessed was able to do unexplainable phenomena like floating in the air, glowing eyes, or float in the water, it's most likely they are just exhibiting signs of psychiatric problems.

You can ask for help and support during the session. Even if you don't call them out, there will be many guides who will be there for your support. But some of them might not be always available. But don't be discouraged if you need their help during the session.

To work with spirits, one doesn't need to be completely unconscious. You can talk to and hear spirits while still being conscious. This is more challenging than just letting them take charge, but certainly safer. You will also learn how you identify yourself later to determine if you have come in contact with a different spiritual entity. You'll also learn how to protect your self during and after contact.

Channeling involves sharpening the psychic senses. For best results, you must continue to enhance your psychic skills. If you don't believe that you are psychic enough, this book will help you learn how to become one.

Contrary what popular belief says, psychic abilities are universal. The degree of psychic sensitivity that people have is different. Some people have psychic gifts from birth, but people can learn how and practice them over time.

Chapter 2: Core Channeling Skills

"The measurement of a conversation will be how many people recognize it and how many people share it. If you only talk about what you think, or don't consider what other people are feeling, you may as well be talking to yourself in a group.

- Dylan Moran

These are crucial skills that you should master before you attempt to channel.

The channeling of religious beliefs and the belief in channeling

Each belief system has their own channels for channeling specific guides. Eckankar (Order of the Rosy Cross), and Theosophy channel the "ascended masters". Kuthumi is an ascended master that was instrumental in building Theosophical Society.

There are many UFO religions which worship extraterrestrials and claim they can communicate with their members. Catholics may sometimes claim that they have seen apparitions or images of Mary. Edgar Cayce, a channel from Akashic records. These groups and practices are so numerous it would take many books to fully discuss them.

There are benefits and drawbacks to having a belief system you can channel. Many religious groups have scriptures, traditions, or other information to guide their members. They will have extensive information about the entity. It is not necessary to start with nothing when approaching entities that are part of this group.

Religious beliefs can, however, interfere with the reception of the message. Reactions and beliefs that are negative towards one type of being could cloud your ability to perceive it. Sometimes, communication can be hindered by an inability to like or fear another religion.

The bottom line is that while it is simpler to join a team with a system than to explore the unknown solo, it will lead you to receive biased information. It is essential to be objective and reflect on the ways your beliefs can influence how you view or respond to any entity. This is particularly important if you strongly believe in your religion.

Think about your thought patterns. Do you depend more on logic and faith? Do you prefer feel-good ideas more than fearful thoughts? What themes are you drawn to? Take a look at whether the belief system suits your personality. You have two options: you can adjust yourself, or you look for another system. If you don't have the ability to reconcile them, communication may not be as smooth.

After you have decided on a system, stay with it for at minimum a month to get as much knowledge as possible. Even if you don't like the system, starting somewhere will give enough experience that you can use it with other systems. Don't try to learn everything in one system.

The only way to truly learn a system is through dedication. Your dedication to the system may make the spirits more responsive when they hear your sincerity when you call.

You may attract mischievous entities if you're just beginning to study a system. They might pretend to represent someone else and get away because you lack the experience necessary to recognize a true spirit from one that is not.

Receiving the Message

Whatever your preferences may be it is best to strike a middle ground between the extremes. Try to view things with the eyes of someone who demands proof before believing. Look for evidence and reject blind faith. Learn from other people and look for good qualities in them.

Being a channel requires that you prepare your mind for the possibility of containing another person's mind. If your mind is not flexible enough, it might be difficult to connect to another person. Worse, while you may believe that you are speaking for an entity, your biases as well as prejudices can be expressed. If this is true, it's possible to be embarrassed when critics point this out.

Due to the importance of not forcing yourself to make decisions, it is important that you learn how to accept everything that happens during the session. This includes not getting anything.

If you try to make something up, your imagination might override reality and take over. This can be embarrassing, especially if you are able to blurt out details that you keep in your subconscious mind.

These are important for a channel to maintain balance:

Your rationality

Your receptiveness

Your personality

Personality of the entity

It is important to receive the transmission without judgement but also be discerning enough to know when your own ego pretends it is the entity you are channeling.

You must be able to openly allow another entity's thoughts through your mind without resistance from all your beliefs. You should also be able and willing to see through your own beliefs if the message isn't right for you.

These are complicated skills that you may need to learn, but you can practice them daily. Increase your tolerance for ideas and people who are different than you. Learning to be critical will help you spot the lies in others and yourself. Make sure your beliefs, attitudes and actions are helping you channel better than trapping yourself in an unhelpful mentality.

What the channel will send to you will be filtered through your own thoughts. It is essential to avoid biases and be open-minded so you can absorb the information. Exoterrestrials may have different ideas than humans and will therefore try their best to translate it. This may allow you to better understand and express your new ideas.

Communicating the Message

Vocalizing information is dependent on the entity's communication capabilities and partially on the channel. In deep trance states, the channel's channel may not be able to understand what the entity is saying. While in partial trance, the entity can pass ideas onto the channel's brain and the channel may have to make words of them.

It is a plus to be a good communicator. You should work to improve your communication skills. It is crucial to understand how to effectively communicate your ideas verbally.

Here are some suggestions:

Expand your vocabulary

Learn more words. This does not mean that you have to use flowery words to impress your audience. Rather, it is about having something to use for complex ideas.

Creative writing is possible

You will be able to articulate what you think and feel by writing poetry and short stories. Writing creatively also helps you to use your right-brain abilities, which are associated higher psychic sensitivity.

Check out a wide range of literature

Reading can increase your general knowledge. The more information that you have the ability to understand, the better. Find out more on different topics, no matter if they are fiction or nonfiction. However, if your only focus is on a small number of topics, it might be that the information you receive gets filtered out.

Write a journal

You will be able to express your thoughts in a journal, which will help you become more comfortable with the idea of expressing yourself. You will also need to keep a diary in order record psychic impressions.

Talk to your self

Talking to your self brings out your thoughts. Sometimes conversations can take unexpected turn as you speak things you don't realize. It could also be an opportunity to receive a message from a spirit.

You can loosen your personality

Your personality should be allowed to overtake your consciousness and you need to open your heart to the possibility of another being. This ability to be open is one of the most crucial skills you can develop to channel effectively. You need to be relaxed mentally, emotionally, and physically in order for this to happen.

Relaxation of the body

There are two types of relaxation: passive and active. Passive relaxation is when a practitioner, such a masseuse/physical therapist, works on the body. Active forms require that you do exercises and other sports to push your body's limits, and help it overcome its weaknesses. Hatha Yoga can help reduce physical defense mechanisms, increase flexibility, and increase openness.

Recall that relaxation can also mean letting go. It's not ironic, but you might need to be physically active to relax. But, these exercises will also allow for relaxation.

Diaphragmatic breathing

With your back straight, stand or sit comfortably. Place your hands on the sides or back of your waist. Your thumbs should be in your back. When you inhale deeply, gently press your waist into the ground. Begin to inhale by gently pressing your waist into the air.

Feel your waist drop as your diaphragm contracts. Inhale slowly. This type of breathing will increase your lungs' capacity, as well as have a relaxing effect.

Get rid of your muscle tension

Standing straight, raise your arms high. Tighten every muscle in your body. As you relax your muscles, lower your arms to the sides. Continue this movement several times until each muscle is fully relaxed. Pay attention your neck and shoulders. If your neck and shoulders are tight, close them and rotate your head slowly to the left.

Relaxing your mind and body

You can lie on your side. Starting with your feet, relax every part of the body. Allow your feet and legs to become very relaxed. You can continue this upwards with your legs, your trunk, your arms and shoulders.

Emotional Relaxation

Emotional issues can prevent us being receptive. These issues can often be resolved in a variety of ways.

Psychotherapy

Regular psychotherapy can help with emotional blocks and patterns. You should be aware, however, that although common verbal therapies may help to identify patterns and allow you the ability to let go of your emotions, they are not able to do so. This is why cathartic methods like Reichian, Gestalt and Gestalt therapy are more appropriate. Neurolinguistic Programming may be used to change unhelpful emotional response patterns.

Visualizing Calmness

Imagine a beam of healing light entering your crown. Visualize the energy filling your head and lifting tensions. Be aware if you have any emotions stored in it. Let the light bring healing and cleansing to it. Move down slowly while you do the same with the rest of your body.

Mental Relaxation

Habitual beliefs and thoughts can cause mental instability. Psychotherapy is a way to help you recognize hidden patterns in your mind and get out of them.

It can promote a feeling of well-being through vigorous exercise and break negative thought patterns.

Negative thoughts can also be helped by the visualization exercise.

Breathing Exercises

Take deep breaths. Begin to inhale positive emotions such joy, tranquility, and affection. As you exhale imagine feeling negative feelings like anger, fear, stress, and anxiety. Do this for 5-10 minutes.

Meditation is an excellent way to relax and unwind mentally. Next, we will be discussing meditation techniques for improving your channeling ability.

The ability to increase your mental flexibility might be enough to give you insight from another person. This chapter will focus on how to make the most your mind's natural abilities.

Chapter 3: Sharpening You Psychic Sensors

"The precognition and telepathy functions may represent a rudimentary survival mechanism of a power more readily available among animals and primitive human groups than in modern urban civilizations. It is possible to argue that it exists within all of them. However its emergence or development is influenced, sometimes even hindered by, the culture, the circumstances, and the personal histories of each individual. In each case, it is clear that consciousness exists. It has also been proven to be real.

Reginald Omez O.P.

The spirits communicate with us just as clearly as normal people. Sometimes, however, they may only show themselves briefly. These are times that we should adjust to better adapt to their presence.

You should know one thing about mediumship, channeling and mediumship: developing psychic abilities is not the same as being psychically flexible when channeling. Being psychically open is the ability to see and hear things differently than your normal personality. This does not require you to have other psychic abilities.

The best channels are those who are psychically flexible and have learned to be receptive. Psychics have a high degree of psychic flexibility, which allows them to access their potential. This trait is important and must be nurtured.

Psychic Development

Psychics are people that can obtain information through unconventional methods - these include not observing, researching and remembering.

Because it is part if the mind, especially the subconscious mind (everyone has psychic abilities), everyone is naturally gifted with them. Certain people are more likely than others to use them, making them appear more psychic.

The following characteristics of psychics include:

They can get into a trance very easily. These psychic abilities are more apparent in a non-analytical state of mind.

They are more attuned for inner experiences such a visions or dialogues, feelings or thoughts, and so forth.

They grew up in a world that believed the paranormal was acceptable. Although psychic abilities are common in children, their parents teach them to put aside these abilities as people around them are skeptical. These abilities may be encouraged by some homes.

They use the right-brain more strongly. Brain dominance theory claims that the two halves share distinct functions. The left brain hemisphere includes logic, reasoning, sequential processing and language. Science, math, and language are some of its functions. The right brain is involved in intuition, emotions holistic processing, imagination, music, fantasies and imaging skills. Left brain functioning tends toward reducing psychic abilities, while right brain functioning supports these abilities.

Awakening Self-Awareness

You already have the ability to channel your psychic gifts. Being able to recognize and acknowledge them will help channel your energy better. Keep a journal for this purpose. It will allow you to write down any instances where your psychic abilities have been activated.

Here are some examples:

It was possible to make your dreams come true

Visions can be received either while you are awake or during your dreams.

Without the need to say anything, you can still see what another individual is thinking

Feeling the feelings of another person, even if there are no outward expressions

Being a believer in the possibility of something happening, and it did.

Sensations that inform you about something

You must remember that these provided accurate information. Even if you have the wrong intuitions, you may still be able to identify real psychic abilities from your wishes or fears.

True psychic abilities can't be compared to:

Biases

Fears

Hopes

Desires

Expectations

Hallucination

Imagination

These could lead you to believe that things are true. All those times you thought your psychic abilities were real, only to find out that it wasn't. Now think about the reasons you had that hunch. What would you do if something happened to you? Is that what you are afraid of? Are you biased towards this idea? What caused your thoughts and emotions to lead you to make a mistaken judgment?

To be as impartial and unattached as possible to what you see, it is essential that you do your best work. This is why it is so important to mentally and physically relax before channeling any psychic activity.

Trance Walking

Your ability to enter into a trance can be crucial for channeling or using psychic abilities. This is because psychic information can be blocked by the normal state.).

These are just a few examples of times when you may have entered a trance.

Dreaming

A few minutes before falling asleep

The last few minutes of your awakening before you can fully get up

Relaxing deeply

Praying

Meditating

Being sleepless

Being sensory deficient (example, in a darkened room in an isolation tanks)

Being severely stressed/ill

Do you use drugs?

When you sense hallucinations and your inner dialogue is muted, you will know when you are in an altered state.

Remember that psychic abilities do not require you to risk your life.

These are safe, easy ways to get into a psychic Trance.

Sensitivity stimuli should be reduced (dim or turn down the lights, close the eyes, shut the radio, cover your ears, reduce distractions).

Breathe slowly and deeply.

Relax your body

Be still, without straining

Calm yourself down

Be free from worrying thoughts and emotions

Simply put, the physical, emotional and mental relaxation exercises will allow you to go into a trance, and activate your psychic abilities.

Before you use psychic abilities, it is important to clear your mind. You can make any perceptions you want by retaining any emotion or thought. Spend 5-10 minutes relaxing and letting go of all preoccupations.

Receive psychic information

Be sure to wait until your mind is in a trance, before you ask a question or focus on something. This is because you can't focus on something if you are still thinking at your normal level. Trance state allows you to access the subconscious mind of your subconscious, which is where psychic information is received.

Information psychical may appear in the form or symbol of images, symbols, scenes. Sounds, ideas, memories and sensations are all examples. You should pay attention and be open to all that comes your way. Do not force them into appearing in a certain manner to prevent tampering with data.

They should be taken down as soon they are received. Write them down. Don't try to analyze the information that you get.

Stop recording when you don't get anything or you feel like you are forcing impressions.

Interpreting Psychic Information

Although psychic information may seem easy, it is often complicated and multi-layered. This is why you should analyze their meanings.

You must be able recognize when parts of the message are being caused by others - things in the environment or your fears and expectations.

It is important to interpret information based upon all you know. There are no guidelines to interpret because everyone's mind is individual. You can interpret the meanings of dictionaries, but only you can understand what your subconscious mind means.

These should be understood, even though you may not know the meaning.

Later, get more information about your question or goal. Examine where you got the correct interpretations and where your mistakes were.

Eventually you will begin to notice clues regarding what specific psychic impressions may mean.

Your psychic dictionary will help you interpret signals faster.

Methods of psychic development

Many different methods are available to enhance psychic abilities. Sometimes they are developed by simply being present. It could happen when the person studies mysticism more or is surrounded by psychics. A traumatizing incident or any other event that shakes one's preconceived notions about the world can trigger it.

Activating Kundalini

Kundalini (energy at the root of the spine) activates the chakras. When activated, the Kundalini flows along a channel on the spine towards a crown chakra in the skull.

The root chakra refers to an individual's individuality and relationship with material existence. Meanwhile, the crown chakra represents the Universe or spiritual planes. The Kundalini connects with the cosmos energy by rising to meet the crown. This allows him/her to meet God and obtain extraordinary abilities, such as psychic abilities that allow them to enter other realms and ability to communicate with the Divine.

Kundalini Yoga works to awaken Kundalini using meditations. There are many books available on the subject and you can try to activate it yourself. However, it is recommended you learn it under the supervision of an authentic master.

One guru who has awakened the Kundalini of another can also awaken it via energy transference. This may have different effects depending on how spiritually developed the student is. However, the activation can be prolonged by regular spiritual maintenance.

Visualizing your Kundalini climbing up your spine is a simple way to awaken it. Imagine a ball filled with energy at your tailbone. Inhale and see this energy glowing - this will boost its energy. As you exhale imagine the energy moving slowly up your spine.

Slowly go through the motions and feel where it is in your body. This may take several seconds. Sometimes, you may feel unwell or tired and be unable continue. You might stop and go back to the beginning.

Clear the channel so that the Kundalini can ascend more easily. This is why you must first prepare your chakras. If you are looking to awaken your Kundalini in an effective way, there are many guides that will help you.

The Third Eye is awake

The Ajna, or third-eye chakra, is the chakra responsible to psychic abilities. This chakra is located in between the eyebrows and the middle of the forehead.

The energy wheel of the spine called chakras. Each chakra represents a different aspect of someone's life as an entire realm. The third-eye chakra symbolises a person's psychic abilities and is the area where the physical and spiritual planes intersect.

Some people believe that third eye chakra is connected with the pineal. This may be because it is the middle section of the brain. Therefore, thoughts and sensory stimuli could meet at this part. Its structure is very similar to an eye and even light-sensitive. It is responsive to DMT (dimethyltryptamine), a substance that induces visions such as those seen during mystic experiences and lucid dreams.

Zirconium can be found in the pineal cells, making it possible to function as transmitters. Zirconium, which is piezoelectric means that the pineal cell may be capable of converting vibrations into electric impulses.

The pineal system may be the bridge between the real and the virtual worlds. Everything is basically vibration. The pineal gland is able to detect frequencies from different realms, and translate them into something usable. It can also transmit and receive information like a radio.

Energizing the third eye or cleansing the pineal can be done to activate it. Third eye chakra can be developed through energy transference and rituals. Meditation can be guided or it can be done by you. You can also channel energy through your imagination and stir the chakra.

Enter the psychic Trance. Visualize your third chakra becoming brighter.

Third Eye Meditation

Meditation can lead to states of mind which allow psychic abilities and other mental faculties to manifest. You can find meditations specifically made for the third eyes.

Here are some examples.

Humming Vibrations

Because the pineal nerve is piezoelectric it can be affected by vibrations. Sit straight back and comfortably. Close your eyes. The spot at the top of your head should be the level of the eyebrows. Slowly inhale. Exhale slowly and deeply. Imagine the vibrations reaching your temples, forehead and deep into the center of your head.

Pouring Energy

Awareness carries energy. Whatever you focus on, energy will flow to it. Find your third eyes - this can be found by feeling the sensations, an inner knowing or vision. Don't be concerned if you're focusing in the wrong place. The energy will travel to where it is intended to. Imagine pouring your energy into it, until it glows. Indigo-colored light could be used as this is the third eye chakra's color.

Healing the Third Eye Chakra, and Pineal Gland

Sending intention of haling towards your third eye, pineal and other glands can help to heal them. Believe that they will be healed. Having faith can make energy flow more smoothly and doubts can hinder it from flowing. Imagine your third-eye becoming clearer, more vibrant, and healthier. Visualize the healing light entering at the center of your forehead. Imagine the light cleaning the chakra.

Take care of the Pineal Gland

Although it isn't yet certain if the pineal hormone is responsible for psychic abilities it may be worth taking the following steps:

Fluoride intake should be decreased

You should check to see if the food you eat and the products that you use contain fluoride. This substance can harden or calcify the pineal cells. You can choose fluorideless alternatives like fluoridefree toothpaste. You can drink and bathe in fluoridated water. You should treat your water first to prevent this ingredient from being added to the drinking water supply.

Take Calcium Supplements Away

Excessive calcium is deposited in your pineal gland. Follow the recommendations of a nutritionist to ensure you are getting the right amount. Supplements are not necessary unless you have a medical reason to.

Detoxifying

These substances can cause damage to your brain, body, and pineal gland. These ingredients may be purified by fasting or going on an elimination diet. Avoid eating unhealthy foods and using harmful substances such recreational drugs, alcohol, and nicotine. Reduce refined sugar intake and eliminate caffeine as much possible. To keep the pineal gland healthy, it is important to keep your body clean.

Pineal Gland Foods

Certain foods are thought to make the pineal system healthier by strengthening and cleansing it. Iodine-rich meals reduce fluoride's impact and make it less likely to build calcium deposits on your tissues. You can find iodine in fish, seafood, broccoli, and other foods. Beets contain boron. This element counteracts calcium. Malic Acid, found in apple cider vinegar, detoxifies metals. Raw chocolate stimulates pineal gland activity and helps detoxify it. Spirulina & chlorella are good options to get rid of mercury in the brain and body tissues.

Sunlight

The sun is the best light for your pineal gland. Spend 20 minutes under mild sunlight. Directly look at the sun for a few moments after sunrise, or just before sunset.

It is not clear that the pineal hormone is directly connected to the psychic abilities of the third eye chakra. If the pineal gills develop tumors, they can be removed without affecting anyone's consciousness. To take care of the pineal system, it is important to have good health. It's not about being sick, but rather, having a healthy body and mind will help psychic functioning.

Third Eye Chakra - How to Develop

The third-eye chakra is just 1 of the 7 major chakras. The state of the chakras can influence what type of experiences you have, and vice versa. It is essential to take care your chakras, so that you attract positive experiences and minimize negative experiences.

The chakras have a direct relationship to each other, so the effects of one chakra on another will be felt by those below it and above. The

Kundalini is able to climb higher and improve their psychic abilities by taking good care of its chakras.

Traditionally, you should work your way up from the lowest chakra. This is because the lower one serves as the support for it. Although it is beneficial to work on all your chakras, rather than just the third eye, psychic abilities can still be used if you are able to.

Problems, traumas and unhelpful thoughts, emotions or suppressions can cause disruptions to the energy flow in the chakras. Chakra issues can be solved by dealing with the cause of the problem, and healing the chakra via meditation and visualization. A chakra healer can use energy for clearing blocked chakras, strengthening weak chakras and reducing the activity of overstimulated.

Here are some strategies you can use to create your third eye chakra.

Crystal Healing

Crystals have frequencies that are associated with particular realms. They are used for many purposes: to attract wealth, improve self-confidence, foster relationships, connect with the Divine, and so on. Crystals are associated the chakras. Meditation can strengthen those chakras.

You can use any type of indigo or violet crystal to help the third-eye chakra. You can use lapis, sapphire or sodalite as examples.

Holding a crystal is a good way to meditate. The crystal can be placed on your forehead. You could imagine the energy from it entering your head. If you're not in the mood to meditate, you can keep it in a bag or pocket. You might also place it where you'll be for long periods, such at your desk or beside your bed.

Use affirmations

Affirmations simply consist of simple statements to program your subconscious mind to create positive changes and effect reality via law of attraction. There are many affirmations that promote psychic ability, but you have the option to create your own.

The following characteristics are important for affirmations to be good:

Short

Direct

Simple to understand

Positively formulated (without not and no's).

As if they are already happening (ex. It is not "will get stronger" but rather "growing stronger")

Believable

Gives positive feelings

To be able for your mind to accept and believe in what you are affirming, it's essential that you believe it. You can modify it to make it easier for you to accept. "I choose let my psychic abilities grow stronger."

Your affirmations should be repeated as often as possible, while you visualize it happening. It's better to say your affirmations while you're still in a state where you can receive them.

These are some examples for affirmations you could use:

My third eye is becoming more clear and stronger every day.

I choose that my psychic abilities be used in a positive way.

I'm ready to receive psychic guidance right now.

I now have a connection to my spirit guides.

My awareness grows of the spiritual worlds.

I and all of the cosmos exist together.

I am one in my Higher Self.

I see reality.

Each day my psychic skills become more precise and reliable.

Dreams come true

The ability to work with dreams will improve your psychic skills. Your subconscious mind will speak the language of your dreams and you will be able handle non-physical realms. Recall your dreams, and then reflect on their meaning. It's possible to receive messages from the spirit in your dreams.

Lucid dreams, also known as being conscious in a dream state, allow you to direct what happens in your dream. This will provide you with the opportunity to travel to other worlds and speak to spirit beings.

Lucid dreaming also has many other benefits.

Gathering information

Problem Solving

Practicing skills

Enhancing creativity

Recovering from trauma

You can entertain yourself

You are more self-aware

You must realize that you dream while you dream in order to be lucid. This requires you to develop a high level awareness.

Make a list of all your dreams immediately after you wake up. Do not wait because 90% of your dream could be lost in as little as five minutes. Write down everything you can recall without changing or omitting details. Don't forget feelings, thoughts and sensations.

Keep a record of what you remember from your dream. After a few weeks, you'll begin to notice certain themes or elements that are recurring in the dream. Choose from one to three of the "dream signs." Tell yourself that whenever these dream signs are encountered, you will always remember that it is you who is dreaming. Example: "I will instantly realize that I am dreaming each time I float on the air."

Reality testing is something you can do while you're awake. Reality testing is about determining whether you are still in the ordinary world or if something is happening in your dream.

These tests may be used for some purposes:

You can't turn the lights on, but they will work in a nightmare.

Pushing your arm through a wall, your hand could go through in your dream

Walking through a brick wall. If you wish to dream, it is possible to go the other way.

Imagine looking at a clock and seeing jumbled numbers.

Reading something can cause nightmares.

Gazing at you hands will make your hands look bizarre in a dream.

If you look in the mirror, you'll see something unusual.

Jumping up -- You could fly away if done in a vision

These will become your habitual way of doing things, and you will do it in dreams. When you do this, you might start to realize that you could be dreaming. This will activate the awareness necessary to make it possible for you to control the dream.

It is recommended that you study and master lucid visioning to become a better practitioner of working as a spirit without a human body. A lot psychic work is simply that: being a spirit, and interfacing with other spirits.

Get Aware Of Synchronicities

Synchronicities, or meaningful coincidences, are thought to be the result the mind's interactions of reality. Your mind will become more aware and can see deeper truths if it is less influenced by preconceptions. The synchronicities can help you see the bigger picture and give you insight. Everything is interconnected in a spiritual realm. If you contact the spirits through direct communication, they may also respond through your experiences in life.

Increase your Self-Awareness

You must have a high level of self-awareness in order to gain psychic information. Because the mind has a tendency to filter out material which is contrary to its beliefs and preferences. You must be able to tell the difference between what and how you are hearing it. Reflection should be done every day. Find out the thoughts and emotions that you are thinking, and what they are causing you to feel.

Figure out why and how you will do it again. Get a sense of the core of you that has not changed over time. It is important to think about the things you are most passionate about, how your views of reality change, what your beliefs are, and other aspects that affect your perceptions.

As a Part of a Whole, See Yourself

To increase your senses of sensitivity, it is necessary to give up your sense of separation. The spirit of all beings is the same - it allows for information and energy to be transferred between them. Accepting this connection will help you develop your psychic abilities and channeling abilities more naturally.

This implies that you should be more flexible, understanding and kind-hearted. You must be able see that other people are just as important as you are, regardless of your feelings towards them. This will help you become more open and more reliable as a psychic.

Your psychic abilities can be used

Increase the use of your psychic skills to make them stronger. But ignoring them can make them less important. Regular practice is necessary to develop a mind that can sense psychic messages.

Stop relying on your normal methods of gathering and sending information. Find ways to get psychic information and to use your psychic skills to share it.

To avoid psychic information being mixed up with your own beliefs, calculations, or sentiments, you need to be able to stay disciplined. The process of using psychic abilities requires a lot more trial and error. But, you will gain more insight into your psychic abilities over time and will be able better to use your psychic talents consistently.

Meditation for Psychic Abilities

Meditation basically involves controlling your mind to direct your attention and energies. There are many meditation practices, but most of them involve an altered state in consciousness.

Find a place that you can meditate in peace for 5-20 minutes without interruption. It is possible to lie down or sit, but it is best to be still so you don't fall asleep. Keep your eyes closed and your attention focused inwards. Pay less attention in the immediate environment and pay more attention to what you perceive in your own mind. Deep breathing is a great way to relax.

Deepening The Trance

To communicate with the spirits of the dead, you can enter a trance and tap into your psychic abilities.

Here are some tips to help increase your awareness.

Counting

Count to the nearest number. Visualize the number in the mind. Encourage yourself to get deeper as the numbers shrink. Example: 100... 99... 98... My mind is getting deeper...97...96...95... I am starting to get into a trance...94...93...92... And I am getting more relaxed...91...90. My mind and body are totally relaxed.

Relaxation through Visualization

Picture something that you find relaxing such as a picturesque scene in the countryside. Also, imagine yourself climbing down a stairs, a ladder, sliding down a slope. If you prefer, you can pretend you are in an elevator that is slowly ascending or an escalator.

The psychic trance is when you reach 1 or the bottom level. Take a look at what you are seeing, but don't analyze it. To avoid being in the same situation again, you should be familiar with it.

This affirmation could be used as a program to enter the trance in the future.

"This is my psychic dream. I can enter this state quickly if I want to use some of my psychic skills."

Feel free modify the words as you wish.

Internal Images

Close your eyes. Imagine a blank white screen in front. It is possible to project an object such as an apple, or a book onto the screen. It is important to make this item seem more real. Imagine it in three dimensions. As though the scent of it wafts in your air, imagine that.

Try to feel the texture, contours, and temperature of the object as you hold it in your hands. You can make this idea fully real by focusing on it for at least one minute. As you become more comfortable with this practice you will be able to increase the amount of time you think about it.

You can also choose to concentrate on an external object, such a candle flame or picture. Focus on this object for at most two minutes. Gradually, you will increase this time as you practice.

How to Nurture Your Psychic Abilities

Most psychic abilities can be activated by entering a psychic trance. There are additional ways you can help psychic abilities grow.

Believe that psychic abilities are innate. If you are skeptical about psychic abilities or believe they aren't real, your mind will be able to hear you and make it happen. Your mind is more comfortable working in the same way it has been for a long period of time. It will therefore not be motivated to use other functions.

If you believe that psychic faculties are possible, your mind will use less of its resources. Recall times when visions and dreams came true. You can learn more about psychic abilities, parapsychology, and other related topics. Interview channel channels, psychics, or anyone else who is familiar with paranormal phenomena. It's easier to believe it the more you understand it.

Have patience. Avoid biases. They will affect or block any incoming information. If you're impatient, you can make things up to please you. To be more precise, you need to be careful about what you think. Be open-minded. Accept information as it comes.

Be more alert. If you're not attentive, psychic signals might be everywhere. Normally, a person holds beliefs and seeks confirmation of those beliefs. The opposite occurs when psychic abilities can be used. The person must suspend all thought and allow the signals of the mind to speak for themselves.

Utilize all of your senses. The mind can sense psychic material and take other forms. These signals are easier to detect if you have sensitive senses such as sight, hearing and smell. While you're paying attention, explore different sensations. While you're experiencing the world through different senses, do not lose your mind. It is possible to train your mind to become more aware of psychic information in the world and around you.

Be curious instead. Curiosity will open your mind to more information than judgement.

Be calm. You can see everything clearly when you are calm. Your mind may pick up similar memories from strong emotions and interpret things in ways that support them. This may affect the way you gather information.

Consider asking someone else to gather information or channel you emotions if this is something you are passionate about. Meditation for 20 minutes could help you to relax and calm your feelings. To make it less annoying during the session, at least write down what is bothering your. You should take at least five deep breaths.

The psychic mind is able to process information in many different ways. This may lead to confusion. Keep track of all information you receive to help you later organize and analyze your received messages. Tell someone you are channeling to that you will not interrupt the other person as you get and share the information. Later, share the recorded material with him/her and help to interpret it.

Don't forget that it is useless to know the techniques and rituals of channeling if you can not switch to psychic modes. This was the reason that the first chapter dealt with this topic. The next chapters describe how channeling works. These instructions do not constitute a complete guide. You can adapt the instructions to suit your needs or use another technique.

Chapter 4: Guide for Channeling

"Engaging spirits doesn't have to be an elite ability or industry. It is simply being active with All Things. It's in our DNA.

- S. Kelley Harrell

Channeling involves calling out to the spirit, interfacing with the spirit, recording and closing the communication. Let's cover each step.

Preparations

You prepare for a channeling session with preparations by getting ready for the group and planning what to do.

Planning the Session

Spirit channeling involves a lot of work so you will need to be clear about your goals. Who are you looking to communicate with? How would this spirit be reached? How could you tell you have found the right being? Why aren't you doing this session anyway? What are the goals of this session? What are your indications for continuing the session or ceasing it? These questions are answered by studying the spirit/s you want to contact.

You need to be aware that there are two main types or channeling: consciousness channeling and spirit channeling.

Spirit Channeling

Spirit channeling is a popular practice that became very popular in the 19th century. While some are con artists who want to make quick money and become popular, there are also genuine spirit channelers. They could speak truthfully about things they had never heard of or that they couldn't learn from normal sources.

Some sessions were also accompanied, in some cases, by otherworldly phenomena. Scole Experiments can give you some insight into what spirits can do.

Channeling Consciousness

This is a relatively young practice that involves the visualization and manifestation of archetypal symbols. This includes past life characters, metaphors for experiences, representations about psychological trauma, etc. These individuals will interact with them to learn more about themselves and heal psychological injuries.

What kind of channeling do you use depends on whether your goal is to get information from yourself or another being. Sometimes, you don't necessarily have to choose your information source. Your spirit guides may be able to direct you to the right person.

Clarify What You Desire to Know

Make sure you clearly identify your goals, questions and expectations so you won't waste time pondering what to say to the spirit after it is called.

Preparing for Channeling

You know from the beginning that channeling requires openness and receptivity.

These are some things you could do to prepare.

Prepare for strange things

Channeling may seem very routine, or can include surprising events such as sudden thunderstorms and floating lights. Open to all possibilities - remember that your sessions are protected at all times and that there is always a guardian spirit watching over them. You will increase spirits' ability to communicate with each other if you are open and willing to accept whatever happens. But if you insist on a certain outcome, your spirit might not be motivated.

It is possible to expect something that you already know. It's not possible to experience authentic spirit communication. True spirit communication can surprise anyone who hears it. Try to be open-minded and receptive. Listen rather than impose.

Manifestations Of The Spirit

Amazing phenomena can be caused by contact with spirits, such as:

Ectoplasm-A substance that looks like a mucous barrier and which may sometimes be released from its bodily orifices, or appear on surfaces.

Levitations - Furniture, objects, people, and people float in Levitations

Materializations - These are objects that suddenly appear. They may be created by the spirit of the spirit or teleported there from another place. Beyond objects, spirits are capable of materializing to the point that they appear solid.

Spirit raps- The spirits may make noises by knocking on furniture or walls.

Apports: Spirits can bring objects from another plane like flowers, animals or objects.

Voices-- The medium, an apparition, and an unknown source can all produce sounds and words.

Lights: A light can be seen in many colors and shapes.

Breezes- These can be light, heavy, warm, cold, strong or scented.

Musical instruments - Music from musical instruments can be heard even without a radio.

Singing is also possible, even if the source of the sound is not apparent

Tipping/tapping of the Table - Spirits may tap on or move the table.

Scents - Different kinds of scents can emerge from the ground, such as flowers and fragrances, medications, smoke or foul odors.

Spirit photography: Images of spirits captured on film

EVP (Emotional Voice Program) - These are spirit voice messages that can be heard through the TV, radio and telephone.

The above mentioned experiences are only some of the possibilities. Prepare for anything. Be calm, though. Violent phenomena are very rare. Most channels and mediums state that they have never been involved in a dangerous session.

Be prepared for confusing messages

The spirit realm is a vast realm of knowledge that we do not know. It is not possible to expect messages to arrive written in perfect English. It can be in the form of images or memories, sounds, synchronicities and other unanticipated ways. You need to be open-minded that things may not work out the way you want them to. This includes not receiving any response. You need patience. Even though it may seem frustrating, you will be rewarded for your patience. If you do receive responses, they will be more authentic.

You must be serious

A sincere intention behind the activity is what makes psychic abilities work. Your mind must be open and willing to learn anything that is difficult to understand. If you are not ready to process the information, the mind or spirits might filter it out.

Be informed

The more you understand, the better you can control the channeling session. The occult is something you should research. You should know about the spirits and their characteristics. Also, how to summon them. There are many spirits and instructions for calling each one are beyond the scope this book.

When you get into occultism, you will see a lot of symbols. It will help you recognize symbols, which will enable you to understand why rituals are called such and what to do when working with them. Find out as much information as possible about paranormal phenomena, which are things that do not have a scientific explanation. To understand your own mind, and that of other creatures, you should study parapsychology and psychology.

Psychic Diet

It is believed that our vibratory level is affected by the food we eat. Foods have their own vibrations. Some foods are higher in frequency while others have lower frequencies. Gurus advise that people who work with spirits eat high-frequency foods in order to better tune into the spiritual plane.

Low frequency foods will affect perception, making it more difficult for spirits to be perceived. It is important to avoid red meat, even though you are not planning on channeling for the day. These take a long while to digest. For example beef can take as much as 36 hours.

You can find high-frequency foods in fish, white meats, fruits, and veggies. Each day, consume a large amount of fresh fruit & vegetables. It is best to eat them raw as they are more energy-rich. Veganism is a good option for spiritual practices.

Foods with high frequency tend to be those that have not suffered a death before being eaten, foods that were raised in a happy environment that receives plenty of sunlight and food that was natural. Low frequency foods are processed and/or butchered using chemicals. These include red meat, junk foods, and foods containing preservatives.

Fast food and junk food should be avoided if possible. Consume foods low in fat. Avoid cigarettes, beer, and other alcoholic beverages. Anything that is harmful to the body puts it in survival mode. This means that your body will spend more energy healing its own wounds, and you'll have less energy for psychical work.

This is a fact that your body will find a way to conserve its energy. Low energy reserves will prevent you from channeling psychic information or obtaining/sending it.

Even though it's not required, you can fast to purify your body and clear out toxins. If your body is cleansed, your energy body will too. This will increase your spiritual perception. But don't be afraid to not overeat. To reiterate, if your body is in danger, it will enter fight or flight mode.

It is best not to eat within one hour after channeling. If you ate large amounts, wait at the least six hours. If you eat a lot, blood will be diverted to your digestive system. This means that your brain will have less nutrition and blood. It's important not to channel after eating. This will make it hard to focus and deplete your energy quickly.

Exercising for Psychic Development

Exercise has many benefits. You can get better physical health, rid yourself of toxins quicker, be more attentive to your body and have more energy. Exercise at least three days a week. Do gentle exercises before channeling.

Salt Water Swimming

Saltwater bathing can purify the body, enhancing spirit perception. Although this is not a requirement, it might help you channel your energies better. Add 1 cup rock salt to your bathtub. Allow it to sit for 30 minutes. This can also be done after a channeling or whenever you feel that there are negative energies and traumas.

Aromatherapy

Aromatherapy can affect consciousness and enable channeling. Scents influence the vibrations in people and the environment. Some scents attract spirits. You may use oil, perfume, incense and oils. There are occult books which will give instructions on summoning particular spirits. They may also include information about the best scents to use.

Building healthy relationships

The way you relate to other people can impact the way you interact spiritually. Be kind to others. Take part in the life of your family. Be involved with your friends in productive activities. Volunteer to help the poor. Your work will benefit from the positive energy you create.

Purify Your Mind

Everything around a person has an energy equivalent. You can't avoid negative thoughts and feelings. But you can try to forgive others and think positive thoughts. Focus on positive feelings such as joy and love instead of fear, hate, and other distressing emotions.

How to Develop Perception

Chapter 2 was about increasing psychic sensitivity. Here are some other ways to increase your sense of perception.

Use tools

There are tools to help increase your awareness of the spiritual dimension. Some of these include runes (tarot), astrology/numerology, numerology, and even pendulums. These will help to bring you closer into the energies of spirituality, which will make it easier for you to communicate with spirits.

Do Energy Work

You'll be more open to energy work such qi Gong, pranic, healing, Reiki, feng Shui and other forms of energy work. This will help you to be more open to the possibility of seeing spirits.

Spend time in Nature

Modern lifestyles drain our energy. Spending time in nature while enjoying healthy food will help replenish your energy levels and improve your ability to see. Take a trip to the mountains, forests, or oceans. Find a quiet place to meditate. If you meditate often in a natural environment, it is possible to forge bonds with the spirit of nature.

Visualizing to Increase Vibratory Speed

Visualizations work in spirit because energy follows thoughts. You can use imagination to raise your vibratory rates and clear out your senses. Imagine that your body is made up of light. Imagine this light becoming brighter. You'll feel the vibrations increasing in speed until it becomes clear that you can see the high frequencies. Reduce your brightness until it is normal again. This will help you return to your physical reality, and prevent you attracting unwelcome spirits.

Preparing to make Spirit Contact with a Group

It is generally easier for a person to channel than a group. Here are some suggestions on how to prepare group channeling meetings:

It is important to establish a schedule. The date and time when the session will begin are important. Set a time limit for the session. Don't allow it to drag on for hours as you will quickly become exhausted.

Determine who will serve as the channel/medium. The best people for this role are psychically sensitive and highly experienced, but you can train the less-skilled.

Limit the number. Do not invite more than 6-8 people. The spirit can be difficult to manage so try to lessen your burden.

If you don't have to invite someone with problems, it is best not to. Negative experiences could result for people who aren't physically or psychologically healthy. The session will be challenging if you don't prepare well.

You should not include skeptics. They can cause a decrease in spiritual and psychic activity. They may also disturb participants by interrupting what is being done because they don't believe it to be true. They may also be reluctant to talk if they feel rejected.

The energy in the group is crucial for spirit communication. It's crucial that everyone involved in spirit communication helps to establish clear communication without interfering with it or making things more complicated. It is important to choose carefully who you include.

Spirits will listen to those who are present. Some beings will not cooperate if they find out that a participant did something harmful to entities. Informing the participants about the spirits to be contacted before the session. Ask them if it will be a problem for the spirit to have them.

Discuss the nature of your questions and who you will contact. List all questions and their identities. The next chapter will focus on effective questions.

Prepare all the necessary items for contact with a spirit. These may include ritual guides or incense, ritual offerings, candles, and/or offerings. These can be placed at the center or on an altar.

Choose a quiet place that is private with enough seats and a large table. This can be done as a ritual to cleanse and protect the area from negative energies and entities. Incense can be used to clear the place.

Eliminate all distractions. Silence all phones. Turn off all TVs and radios. The space should be as quiet and private as possible in order to not distract others. It is easier for spirits to communicate in a quiet environment. The lights should be turned off or dimmed. The darkening of the room will allow participants to experience an altered state in their consciousness, which allows them to better perceive the spiritual realm. Outside, place a sign that says "Do not disturb". If you would like, tell the door that a spirit communication meeting is ongoing.

You should have your equipment prepared. You might film, record or photograph the session. However, it is important to remember that spirits can drain the energy of your equipment. Equipment can also be damaged. Also, keep spare batteries on hand in case your equipment fails.

Keep healthy snacks, such as candies, close at hand. This will provide energy, grounding, and more. You can make a pitcher with water, but not ice. Ice rattles or makes noises so don't add them to beverages.

Examine what happened at each session. What were the unexpected things you weren't prepared for? Make sure you are ready for the next session.

Chapter 5: Asking Right Questions

"To ask the right questions is half of knowing."

- Roger Bacon

Channeling sessions primarily involve gathering information. It is therefore important that you know how to properly ask questions. Spirits are just like us humans. They will appreciate honesty and sincerity. They won't answer questions that are foolish, unimportant, or dishonest. It is essential that you phrase your questions well.

How you ask the question will affect how you get answers. The implied statements you make in a question will impact how they respond and how you interpret the answers. It is important to do your research and find out exactly what you are looking for before you start channeling.

Avoid channeling until you have chosen a topic, question or theme. You might get random responses. If you don't have a goal when you reach out to a spirit, it might think you're just interested in talking about anything. If this happens, you might be able to talk with the spirit but you might not be able understand its words. It is best to give the spirit something you can focus on in order to make the session more productive.

The messages must be received clearly by you asking questions. Ask questions that provide useful information. It is best to ask questions that you can verify or apply. If you ask vague or unrelated questions, you are likely to receive vague responses.

Your question must be unambiguous. This means your question cannot be interpreted in multiple ways. Simply state an ambiguous query to make it simpler and clearer.

Don't ask a question with too many parts. If you ask, "Will I have more fun at a new college and graduate this academic year?" The spirit may give confused answers as the question deals with two situations. The possibility that you have a better year because you are happier can mean that you won't be as focused on your studies, which could lead to a delay in your graduation.

This is crucial, especially if the answer you're seeking is a yes or a no. You can simplify complex issues by breaking them down and tackling each piece individually.

Make sure your question is specific, but not too exact. Give the spirit something they can do while giving them enough room to offer you more information.

The question should be related to what you intend to find out. If you want to understand what will happen if your job is changed, you should not ask "Will this be no problem?" Even though you may have some problems in life, that does not mean you will not be successful at your new job.

You can certainly elaborate on this spirit, but it's still possible to miss the point.

The question should enable you to act on the issue. Spirits are not dictators, they guide. Instead of asking, "Will I pass my exam?", ask what you are able to do.

Asking whether you must do or should not do something is not an option. This is because it takes away your responsibility. Second, the spirit may answer according their own biases. It can also answer no or yes to something it doesn't mention.

For the question, "Should you date this new person?" The spirit may say yes as it foresees your happiness with that person. While this person may benefit from your kindness, the spirit doesn't warn you beforehand. This spirit encourages selfless sacrifice and will not allow this to happen. It is wiser to ask what happens if the course of action is chosen.

You might even ask questions about a subject. You may ask for what you are not aware of.

Instead of asking about whether it will happen, consider how you can increase the likelihood of it happening (if that's what you want) or stop it from happening altogether (if that's not what you want).

Find out what your opportunities are, and how you can take advantage of them. Know what is preventing you reaching your goals, and what you could do to overcome it.

Avoid making assumptions or asking questions. Example: "How would life with my boyfriend 10 years from now?" is asking for the assumption that you'll be married after 10 year. Even though you may hear the spirit tell you there will be no "you", it might not make sense to your brain because your attention is on the assumption.

Your options are limitless. The spirits will help guide you towards the best results, so keep your options open. Do not ask "How can my studies be supported without a job?" but "What can I do to make my studies more manageable?" Let the spirit tell you.

Avoid biases wherever possible. Be objective and you'll be able to interpret the spirit of others more accurately. If you don't like someone, rather than asking why, you can instead ask what is making him react negatively. Don't ask anyone who has put a hex upon you if you're having financial problems. Instead, ask the spirit of the universe to help with your reflections on the circumstances that led you to financial difficulties and offer guidance for making better money choices.

Don't alter interpretations when you ask someone for assistance. You are there to provide reliable guidance to people who come to you. You can choose to reveal or not disclose information when it might cause more harm than the good. But you must avoid telling lies. Use your words carefully.

The spirits will be suspicious if you try to trick or lie people. They will then avoid speaking to you in the near future. You might attract trickster spirits to do the exact same things to you that you do to other people.

These are just a few tips to help you phrase productive questions. There are different languages used by spirits, so it is easier to ask questions that work for them than for others. It is important to note what works and which doesn't. Do not assume that every spirit will respond the exact same.

Recording the Session

Recording everything that happens will help to preserve important information that has been given to you. You can then check to see if it's real communication. Keep a reminder of the experience. This will strengthen the bonds you have with the spirits. It will also train your mind to make better contact next visit.

Examine what you have written. Is the information accurate and reliable? Did the spirit of this experience help or hinder you? What did the experience feel like? What thoughts were generated and what emotions? Do you feel energized or drained after completing the task?

Even if you are dealing directly with the spirit, it is important to maintain your practicality as well as critical thinking. True spirit guides will never be offended if they are authenticated. They will see that you are trying to keep them safe and not to anger them.

Fake ones on the other hand will expect you to believe them, and they will be hostile if your doubts are not. These people are usually the worst so beware. Do not trust them just because they claim they have this and that high ranking spirit.

Chapter 6: Meeting Spirits

"The encounter of two people is like two chemical substances coming into contact: if they react, they both become transformed."

- Carl Gustav Jung

It's difficult to do psychic work. Your perceptions will be affected greatly by your thoughts, beliefs, memories, preferences, and other internal factors. Understanding your own mind is key to ensuring that your perceptions are not affected by external influences.

Meeting spirit guides or talking to them requires belief in their existence. Without believing they can exist, your mind might not hear them communicating and you may not be able to sense them. For a greater belief in spirit encounters and to talk with others who interact with them, read more.

You don't have to call upon spirits constantly. Spirits may visit you when they are able to give you information. They may also help you feel better by being there.

Channeling isn't as difficult as it seems, regardless of what you see in the movies. It is as simple as entering a psychic state, connecting with the spirit, then listening.

For You

Focus on the inner world and clear your mind. To disconnect from external reality, focus your attention inwards and you will be able to tune into other realities.

Invent a place where the spirit and yourself can speak and meet. Thoughts exist in the spiritual planes. If you create an area for the spirit and soul to meet, it becomes a real one.

Think of a place that you feel safe and comfortable. Place a barrier around the area, such as a metal wall, a forcefield or tall trees. Place a passageway on one side of this barrier. This is where your spirit visitors will be able to enter and leave your realm.

Try pretending you're in this realm. See the area around you. Call the spirit you choose to meet. If you don't know which spirit to speak with, ask for a guide that has specific characteristics. It is important to list what you want and to what extent you need to learn it.

Expect to see someone at the front door. Let the spirit in through the front door. What is the look of the spirit? Are there any aspects of the guide's appearance that stand out? What is its voice like? Does it smell anything? These details could be significant. These details are worth paying attention to.

Start a conversation. Ask about the spirit's name, function, and origins. Let the spirit speak to you. You can ask anything, but you don't have to force it to respond in the way you want.

After you're done with the discussion, if the guide asks you to leave, tell them how you can recognize it. Ask if there is an easier way to reach it. Before saying goodbye, be grateful to the spirit.

In a group

This is the standard pattern for channeling sessions. The occult custom you follow will determine which ritual is required.

Everyone remains silent, whether they are sitting or standing. The session must be completed by the end of the session.

Participants will fall into a meditative mode by following the exercises mentioned in the previous chapters.

If there are rituals for summoning particular spirits, these will be used at this point.

The channel or medium will receive the spirits.

He/she'll say something like:

We are glad to have you join our circle.

We are always available to answer your questions.

Do you want to leave a message for us

Is there anyone you'd like to chat with?

Are you allowed to ask questions?

Are you willing to talk with us?

It may take several attempts to get an answer to a single question. But don't expect it all to happen in one way. The response you get may be variable. It might appear in the medium's/channel's mind, the environment or both. So that you can notice when something happens, you need to have presence.

Even though there might be a lead medium/channel or participant, they may also become a conduit or channel. You should observe if someone starts talking or reacting. He/she may be sending messages.

You shouldn't force the spirit to get in touch with you. If the connection between you and the spirit is not working, it's up to you to make adjustments. You may need a deeper trance or to raise your vibrations. Perhaps something is keeping you from the frequency on the material plane.

If you are successful in spirit contact, it is possible for you to experience intense emotions. To communicate well, you must not become overwhelmed.

Once the session is concluded, please express your gratitude to the spirits. It is possible to offer prayers. These are for all spirits, regardless if they appear. You can now declare that the session is done.

Participants will then be able to discuss what they have seen, heard, felt, thought, and discussed. You can also listen to recordings. It may uncover some things that were not obvious.

The channel/medium might also transmit specific messages to individuals. This should be done only if the private matter is not being discussed with anyone else. He/she could request that the people concerned remain.

Everyone will do grounding activities. This could include eating snacks, talking about everyday topics, or performing a physical task.

Talking with Spirits Outside of Session

Sometimes spirits will attempt to talk with you without you being present. It is possible to enhance your spirit communication skills by engaging in a conversation whenever this happens.

Feel like a spirit is around, or want to know the entities in a particular area? Get into your psychic trance.

Sending your intention is to reach out for these spiritual beings. A prayer can be said or an invitation may be given.

Pay attention and pay attention to everything that enters your consciousness. Can you see anything? Did a color, or an image pop into your mind? Do you hear a peculiar sound? Can you smell a perfume in the air, or do you hear a strange sound? Can you feel electric shocks, light touches or goosebumps? These sensations should be noted. No matter how insignificant they may seem, make sure you write them down.

Close your eyes. Have a meaningful conversation with the spirit/s. Ask simple questions.

What is your nickname?

Is there anything you can do that will make it easier?

When can you make me notice you more?

How can you be identified?

What is the most important thing I need to do right now?

Do you have something to say to someone?

Please show me your body.

What is your purpose

Where are you most often staying?

Keep a list of all the thoughts that come to your mind. Simply let the words flow. Grammar, spelling and other superficial things are irrelevant. It's not important that you lose the information.

Don't reread what you wrote, even if you are still communicating. For communication to continue, you must remain open-minded and receptive. Keep the analysis for later, when you are back in your normal mode.

A simple closing ritual can be performed at the end. Thank you to the spirits that spoke with you.

Do some exercise or eat something healthy to help you ground yourself.

Some tips for sending messages

Let communication flow naturally. Do not try to make it happen or dictate the direction.

It's okay for things to move slowly. Do not stop until the channel of communication becomes stable.

Don't have preconceived notions. These will block you from thinking clearly.

Minimize questions. Decide what questions to ask so they can give you the information you need. Too many questions can frustrate some. You will find it tiring to continually search for answers.

The session should not be left to spirits. You can access the communication channel anytime you like. Not all spirits are capable of controlling themselves.

Be sure to clearly describe everything before you attempt interpretation. It is important to accurately relay the information you have received. Interpretation is done with the reasoning mind. It is not the same as the psychic mind. Your beliefs and biases will affect how you interpret the message so be aware.

Make your decisions. Do not try to distract spirits by trivial matters. If you do this, the spirits might decide to remain away from you.

Guidelines

Keep your spirits away. If they don't want to talk, just leave them. If you make them angry, they might ignore you more or lash back.

You should not be afraid to channel your inner seance or initiate a seance. Fear can cause distortions in perception and make you more vulnerable.

You need to have a strong and sincere desire. It is possible to touch the spirit and make anything happen. You might regret it later if this is something you do for fun or to force someone else to do it.

Spirits may attach themselves to the medium or channel. It is necessary to ground yourself after each session. You can then visualize cutting any cords.

You shouldn't be alarmed if you are surrounded by strange phenomena. You won't be afraid to listen to a foreigner speak their language. Spirits communicate differently. Don't be alarmed, even if spirits touch and touch you. The protection guides will ensure your safety.

Avoid touching and shaking channel mediums or channel channels while they are in deep trance. This will not only disorient the medium/channel, but it may also affect the energy dynamics.

You may also be able to see spirits if you have physical contact with someone seeing and talking to them. To keep good relationships, be clear about your intent and get permission to do so.

Asking the spirit for specific information is a good idea. A clear message will be more convincing than one that is unclear but is still applicable to many.

Spirit sessions are not always easy. Sometimes there's no spirit activity or information, and other times it can happen. No matter what, take some time afterwards to assess the events.

In deciding whether or not you tell participants about what is happening, use your own judgement. Some things are better kept private, at the very least for the moment. This is especially important when the message is likely to cause devastation among those who hear it.

Never ask participants or clients for permission. Be as objective as possible and don't tell them things that would make them feel afraid. You must be as objective and fair as possible.

Do not speculate or judge. As it is, don't add or subtract from the information unless absolutely necessary.

Do not force contact. There are many factors involved in the opening of the doors to spirit realm. There are times where you can channel easily and other times when you cannot. Keep doing what you can right now.

Some phenomena might not be caused only by spirits. Have discernment.

It is possible for your participants to report experiencing and seeing things that others may not. Keep this in mind. Witnessing genuine spirit phenomena is not possible by just one person. It will happen to many. If the participant's ability to sense spirit phenomena isn't proven to be accurate repeatedly, then there's a possibility that he/she could be hallucinating.

Avoid confusing your mental chatter for spirit communication. Try to separate your thoughts from those you receive.

Other present people may be able to telepathically communicate with them. It's important to be able to communicate with others so you have an idea of where your thoughts are coming.

Don't share what happened with random people. They may not fully understand. They might join you in mocking or debunking your beliefs.

For those who are interested in learning and working with like-minded persons, it is a good idea to join a study group. You can work independently, but you'll be able to learn much faster if others are involved.

You can cry!

Scrying is the use of an object such at a crystalball, water bowl or blank piece of paper to see things that are not physical. This is not necessary for spirit communication, but it will help to familiarize yourself with the visual aspects of your mind's eyes.

The tool should be in front of you so you can see it easily. Because it's easier to catch faint glimmers, it's a good idea that the lights be dimmed or turned off. But visions may also manifest in your mind.

Intentionally or consciously keep the question or thought in your mind. Ask the spirit. Keep your eyes open and gaze at the object. Pay close attention to the objects. Don't let disappointment stop you from seeing something.

If you use a crystal ball to observe clouds or fog, it is possible to notice them. You might also see colors, flashes. Images, faces, and scenes. There are books that can explain these visions. However, it is often enough to consult your intuition to understand what visions are.

Scribing will become easier if you improve your ability to see images within your mind. Try something artistic. Write stories, and picture them coming to life. Visualize often.

Grounding

Grounding simply means to bring yourself back into the frequency of normal reality. The practice of grounding is recommended by practitioners to avoid feeling disoriented or scattered in the spiritual realm. It protects you from unwanted spiritual influences as you remain focused on your day.

To ground yourself, imagine that roots have been planted deep within the earth. Walking barefoot, or any other movement that requires you to move your feet, will also help.

Once you've given up on the spirit, eat something or drink something. This will bring your physical awareness back to the spirit. To avoid feeling dizzy, don't eat a lot. Eating fruit or biscuits is okay.

Building Relationships to the Spirit

Establishing a spiritual relationship is similar as establishing human relationships. The amount of care and time that you invest in the relationship will have an impact on its quality.

Chapter 7: Protecting Yourself

"Let discernment and mistakes be your teachers.

- T.F. Hodge

Experienced mediums and channels say that they have not met troublesome entities during years of practice. There is nothing to worry about.

These are just a few ways you can ensure your peace of Mind:

Wearing amulets

Protective sigils

Visualize white light

Recite a prayer to receive protection

Calling on protector spirits

Assemble a shield and program it for positive spirits to enter.

Some people suggest that you should not use any defensive measures, like flaming swords or destructive spells, when dealing to the spirit.

What would you do if you were to have a conversation with a stranger with a large weaponry? You can protect yourself but not make it intimidating to spirits, especially if they are non-combative.

As you become more aware of spirits, you will be even more noticeable to them. Some believe that psychics who are awakened have a brighter perception than entities, which makes them more attracted to them. It is possible that you will see strange things more often. If this happens, it's better to be curious than afraid.

You can ground yourself if the spirit realms overwhelm you. Befriend people who have doubts about spirits. Stop reading occult and esoteric books. Avoid communicating with psychics through other mediums. It can increase one's psychic abilities. Get involved in activities that don't involve the paranormal.

Be mindful that even if fear makes you feel scared, it is possible for spirits to not wish you to feel scared. Fear is a normal response. Transform your fear and anxiety into love and understanding. It is not necessarily evil, just because it looks strange.

Your spiritual strength must be maintained so that you don't fall for the temptations within the spiritual realm. Protector guides are available, but it is up to you to protect yourself. It is important to not ignore issues that you have. You must work towards resolving them. Bad spirits may profit from your weaknesses. You might be weakened by certain entities to hurt you or control.

You shouldn't be concerned about this. It is possible to learn so much from any experience of trouble. It is possible that the higher spirits have planned it in order to strengthen your spirit. Keep doing what you can and believing that everything happens for the greater benefit of all.

Be discerning. Do not be intimidated or scared of what you see. It is important to know that valid information can be verified. Don't be satisfied with vague and ambiguous information. Ask for clarifications if something is unclear. Good spirits that are authentic will be more than happy to give you details or answer any additional questions. Other sources and the actual events as they occur will also confirm authenticity.

Negative entities communicate aggressively or can make communication difficult. Talking with them and having them around can cause stress, discomfort, and even death. You must be more alert during times of trouble as they are more likely to visit you.

Joining a meditation group or psychic development class will help you accelerate your progress. You should research the group thoroughly to learn more about what they do, and how they treat other members. Be aware that rumors of wrongdoings may be true.

Your wellbeing should not be sacrificed in order to please a group. A group that empowers you will make you more valuable than making you a slave to its members. If you don't feel comfortable with the other members, find one who is. Avoid cult-like behaviour; it is not necessary for spiritual work.

Pay attention if the group requires you to do these.

Promises a lot but doesn't deliver.

Demands absolute obedience

Discourages questioning

Forcing you to take action or make a decision without giving you any time to think

Makes questionable claims about itself

Separates from you, family, and friends

Drains you

This makes it easy to complete tedious tasks

Tolerates rude behavior

Humiliates you

Does not respect privacy

Does it want you to make dramatic changes in your environment or yourself?

Do not accept the answer "No"

Ex. You are entitled to it. It's good for yourself, part of tradition, etc.

There are many organizations that manipulate people using the paranormal or occult. Keep in mind that you are joining the group for your own benefit and not to help others. You have the freedom to leave or join any group you choose.

Keep your body and mind healthy. Being a channel requires you to also work with spirituality - this requires more effort than focusing only on the material. Keep learning about the spirit so that you are ready for whatever may come your way.

Take the time to meditate. Meditation can have many benefits. You will be able to sharpen your psychic senses and more likely to have mystical experiences. Regular meditation will improve your ability to do mundane and psychic tasks.

Don't go to spirit too often. This is a very energy-intensive activity that can lead to exhaustion. This can lead to a variety of symptoms, including a greater likelihood of getting sick frequently or feeling tired more frequently. You may struggle to distinguish reality from fantasy. You may feel lost and disinterested in certain things in your life.

If you feel that your occult activity is interfering your life, it's time to get out of it. Your spirit is affected by the things you do each day. It's not worth trying to be a channel for someone who is having trouble with other aspects. If you don't do the right thing, your spirit may stop interacting with you.

The act of counseling others involves being a channel, medium, psychic worker, etc. It is strongly recommended that you obtain counseling training. Learning how to communicate information to others and getting information from the spirit is just half of the battle.

You must be able communicate your message in a way that empowers the receiver to use the information in a useful and productive way. Many people visit psychics because they have problems, not because of curiosity about the spirit.

Be responsible. You shouldn't channel too much. They may be more dependent on you than they are able to do it themselves. Do not dictate to them what they should do or make decisions for them. You can only communicate, interpret, and receive information. But you must not be a director. You must remain detached and objective.

You can make someone's lives better or worse just by what you say. Remember, the spirits are watching. If they discover that you took advantage someone or that you aren't responsible with their messages, they might not return to you.

False Channeling

It is always a smart idea to 'test spirit' to avoid being fooled by false channeling. The channel's subconscious mind or ego could appear to be a separate entity. Sometimes, the channel might show signs of his/her past personality. These cases are often not positive because they cause confusion and internal conflicts.

These are the questions you need to ask to ensure that communication is genuine with an entity

Is the spirit living up to my expectations?

Does it live upto the standards set by channeling

What is the quality and reliability of the message? Is this reasonable for the type entity you summoned to which it is?

Is the message clear, or vague?

Does the message sound like what the channel thinks? Some people will pretend they are channeling an entity so that they can express themselves, without being held accountable.

What was the reaction of the entity to being asked to clarify its message?

Is this information different from what was presented by the entity or other channels who were involved with it, or is it contradictory?

Is it giving vague prophecies? If this is the situation, it could only be a form intimidation.

Are you being asked to accept communication from the entity because it is of "high-status" - even if that is not confirmed yet?

Are you in a suitable condition to channel that entity? Pure spirits won't agree to be channeled by someone who has questionable morals. The spirit might be fake if the pairing is unlikely.

Is the channel necessary? High-level entities do not need to be channeled.

To contact a specific type of spirit, you need to first read the entire document. Then you can call it correctly and find out if the right spirit has arrived. Also, it is important to learn how to banish the spirit from your contact if things don't go according to plan.

To learn what to expect from the spirit, you have to listen to other people's experiences. They can interact with each other beyond the channeling session. If you ask them to influence your life or if they become close to you, you might be able to have an impact on the events in your own life. You need to be prepared for communication with spirits.

Direct Verbal Channeling

Direct verbal communication is similar to mediumship. To allow the spirit to speak through the channel, the medium and channel must temporarily step aside.

Mediums and channels can learn this skill by working with one entity. This allows them to build a stronger connection to gain greater knowledge over time. It is possible to form an intimate bond with the spirit when it is similar to the channel. It is also possible that they may have a relationship or contract in the past or in other realms.

Others channels may work with many spirits. Multichannel channels can give you more information, but they might not be as thorough or as detailed as the one that is provided.

There are also channels that work with a collective wisdom of a number of guides. They may send one of their representatives to speak on behalf of them. Some representatives may serve as bridges between entities and groups.

The skills of those involved with the communication and the nature or information being transmitted will have an impact on the quality of communication.

Direct verbal channeling often entails trance states. The channel will relax so that information is not impeded by his/her personality. The channel is partially conscious but mostly unaware of many things.

Channels will often only appear to be in a slight trance. This increases the likelihood of distortion, as the channel's personality could affect the message's expression. However it is usually healthier because the channel can use both rational thought and intuition. A channel's self-control is also stronger, so they can direct the session the way they want.

While in trance, some channels may experience a significant personality change. They might have different voice qualities than normal. They might discuss things they are not used to discussing. The appearance of the spirit can be quite different. It may appear as though they are covering the physical face of the channel.

While they may not exhibit such extreme phenomena, some people are able to feel a connection to a spirit even if they do not have these kinds of abilities. These are those who have a high level of sensitivity and control on their own personalities.

You shouldn't assume that the channel speaks and looks normal. People can also fake being possessed by manipulating their voice and altering their actions. Some people may also be suffering from mental disorders such as dissociative disorder and hysteria. The most reliable way to know if spiritual communication has occurred is not to examine the channel's behavior, but the content or quality of the message.

Everybody who deals with paranormal phenomena and the occult needs to be seen by a psychiatrist to maintain their health. This does not mean they will lose their minds when they deal with spiritual forces. But it does help to ensure that psychiatric conditions are not misunderstood. It allows the person to improve his/her mental health and exercise more control over it.

Being able to understand one's inner thoughts will enable the channel to differentiate between their thoughts and other beings. This will make it easier to reduce the distortion of the message. Regular meditation and contemplation about one's own thoughts and feelings, as well their reasons, is a good idea.

Know your patterns of behavior. You must know your habits and why someone notices them. Channeling might cause the spirit's personalities to leave traces, so it's important not to channel it. This isn't necessarily a problem. Some people feel compelled to share their positive qualities with another person.

Chapter 8: Mediumship

"Empathy is about being in someone's shoes, feeling with their hearts, seeing with their eyes, and standing in that person's shoes." Empathy can be hard to automate and outsource. But it is a great way to make the world a better.

- Daniel H. Pink

Mediumship can be described as merging with someone or something to the point where one feels like the other. It is considered the first use of a psychic ability by an individual because babies often perceive themselves as one with the mother. This makes it possible to have some experience with mediumship.

Mediumship refers to the ability of becoming your target. Instead of seeing it as an outsider's view, you can embody it. It may be difficult to see the world from your own point of view, but it will allow you to gain insight that you never would have considered otherwise. It is believed that mediumship can be achieved with a high degree by channeling results through a high degree attunement.

When you get to know your target from its point of perspective, you'll be able to gain valuable insights. You'll learn how it views themselves, what are their needs and wants, the things it has been through, and even what they're planning.

In addition to merging with a target entity/individual, you can also combine with abstract concepts such as an idea and a system. You can also become a person and ask questions about a relationship to study it. It is possible to be part of a group and evaluate its performance. You can feel the relationships between members.

Mediumship is similar in many ways to channeling.

You can see the plans of somebody else from his/her viewpoint.

Discover how people or entities see you

Be able to sell or persuade others

To create change

To be able to experience the dynamics in a cohesive way

To evaluate all kinds of targets, including physical and non-physical.

To understand what another person/group is doing

To choose the right language or actions to use so your target responds in the way you want

To change your past

To understand your futur

To feel what someone else feels

To heal your past self

To help someone talk with someone absent

To assess the needs and wants of another person

To learn a skill you don't already possess

Mediumship is basically about putting yourself in the shoes of another person. This is a common activity and you may not even notice that mediumship is being practiced when you try to understand someone. It is possible to be more aware that mediumship can occur if you are able to see your own self clearly.

Mediumship can be described as a state of mind where you do not judge the information and simply accept it as it is. Some people may lose control of their thoughts or the environment, and may forget a lot about what happened. It's crucial that you keep a record of the session. Keep a notepad or pen and some paper handy.

Mediumship requires that you let go of your ego barriers. The ego can be defined as pride.

To do this, it is necessary to become fully yourself. You must be aware of the moment. You can stop thinking and just observe.

Explore deeper without trying to justify the experience. Who are they? What's your feeling? What's going on inside of you? What are YOU noticing right now What would you like to discuss? What are your most important current events? What do you still hold on to from the past? Are you avoiding the following? Learn as much as you can about yourself.

Now, imagine that you are now your target. It is important not to dwell too much on this. You are now able to act, look and feel like it. It's where you are now. You know what it feels like to be there.

Let the information flow as it is. Noting what you hear is important. You might not remember it later.

When you're done with your work, you can bring your self-respect back to life. Keep in mind who you truly are, your values, and the things you can't live without. Visualize cutting off any ties with the target. If you don't do this, you will begin to assume their characteristics. This will cause you to behave and think in a similar way.

Keep in mind that, although we are all the same in spirit, we still have individual identities. Each person has a unique job that no one else can do. Even if other people have the ability to communicate, merge, and connect with your mind, it is still your responsibility to do so. The experience should enrich rather than diminish your personality.

Changing beliefs

I have already said that it would be akin to you wanting freedom from prison. Public opinion, religion, or national ideology has been based on fear. This fear includes fear of the unknown. People who haven't dealt with their inner fear are often unconsciously trying support these fears among others. You could argue that the history, religion, politics and culture of the world are all human creations.

It will not be difficult if there is self-confidence, belief and understanding. For those who fear so much that they feel sick, or have difficulty sleeping, learning channeling... can help. Understanding that fear is not a mental construct, and that it is often artificially maintained within society, is crucial.

Be energetic

Channeling has nothing in common with yoga teachers or reiki masters. Even if you have been involved in energetic matters before, contact to higher dimensions will require a totally different energetic preparedness. Practice and previous attempts will help. Meditation is great for the start of the channeling process. This is why it's important to have a sense of readiness, be patient and take things step by step until you can see the end result as clear and simple.

Because of past emotional trauma and fearful beliefs, the human energy field is usually very dark. An individual has lost the courage and ability to advocate for himself, and they are surrounded by sorrow. Their energy is stronger and emits more positivity than other dimensions. It instantly transforms and changes the darkened energies in the person. They are resisting to change. Due to the influence of much more powerful energy, they will begin to emerge like a centrifuge. This could also be called energy cleansing.

If such powerful energy enters the human body, it can cause a physical reaction. These symptoms are all very similar but may vary depending on each individual's level of preparedness.

Your spiritual guides, the angels or aspects, will know the best way to deal these feelings. It is vital to express your gratitude by saying "Yes! I choose this!" Yes, yes, I want these changes to happen in me!" But before you do that, it is important to stop rushing and ask yourself, "Is this really what I want?" Life will always make it the way it's supposed to be.

Mental preparedness

It's an interesting topic. I can instantly tell how your mind should look - it looks like a blank paper! If someone says "I know what I want (something), because firstly... then... and thirdly ..."", it is just an automatic building of the mind. If someone says that they need it to be able help others, then it's not in their heads. If you believe that someone should get help, then it is likely that you need to help yourself first. How did you come to the belief that things are not as they should be?

Sometimes people will say the reverse. There are many thoughts in the head that can distract from what one needs. All of this can be channeled when you are ready.

I call them "knots". Someone with a strong Ego may declare they want to communicate only using the highest energy. It is likely, however, that the person will be confronted with an energy overload situation that will free them from their preconceptions and make them more open to possibilities.

If we learn to meditate and "turn on" the minds, we can both hear and understand what is being said by our mind. I discovered meditation helped me achieve the state of being completely free from thoughts. It is something I have been able to keep up with on a daily bases since then. On this "empty back ground", I quickly saw what the mind "in action" looks. People get mad and believe they are smarter or better than others. They blame each other. And they don't even know the source of the idea, which suggests they "know so many things". The darkness is like a black background, but the light can show you the tiny details of each color.

It doesn't focus on "good" or evil, but instead shows an example life in the noises of the mind without clear vision. As though the mind were a blank page, every smaller wave that passes through our minds can be spotted and thought of as "Hmmm... interesting. I wonder who it is who thinks such thoughts right now."

Channeling can help us overcome the mental block if we are still in it. Spiritual beings often state that the red color in our aura creates the self-image. This is why it takes some time before the red color is fully processed. I asked a close friend of mine a question that he was interested in, and not another. Here's what my friend asked me: "What do I need to do to make money?"

It was actually quite strange, because I could see his tiny mind, fearful, saying, "You need pursue, achieve, and you need something else. This is how we can quickly test ourselves, asking, "Why do you have it?" With such "interrogation", you can find out your true needs, or determine if it's just another mental noise.

I'm repeating: the more empty your "page", you are better! We don't have any obligation to save the world, help or acquire any ability. Because everything is perfect, there is no need to be a burden on ourselves. As perfect as it is possible! If we tell ourselves that we know how things should go and that it is better than the current situation, then that means we wish to have a new life. There is no "wrong" experience. Therefore, everything is perfect.

Here is an example showing what happens to a person whose mind is not yet ready for channeling.

"What? Channeling? Me? Now? Immediately? It is not necessary. Etc.... "

Here is a mind ready to channel:?Hmm ..... interesting ..."

If the mind is blank and there are no "whites,blacks, warm", very good, good or bad, wise, stupide, large, small, don't want, need, desire, or want", then it can be the best.

Channeling is essential

This is where the fun and best part begins! Why should I experience channeling? If a person is at home watching TV, no questions are raised. Someone might feel completely satisfied but another person might still question it. This is what we call a "natural curiosity", and can be broken down into three categories.

1. A need - An inner need, the desire to channel.

2. You have a true need to channel this energy and do it from your heart.

3. A curiosity - a natural curiosity about what channeling can be.

These are the conditions which "give permission to receive information" through channeling. Human minds are not capable of understanding the distinction between a need and a whim. This and that are totally different things. Similar, the thoughts of the soul and the actions of the consciousness are two different things.

What is an "interest"? Interest can be described as an inquisitiveness of joy or curiosity to discover new things, become familiar with them and "play with" them. For small children, it's a natural curiosity to find out everything about the world.

Did you notice the change in writing style? Matt suggested that I continue because he was getting bored with my thoughts. As you can see, channeling works as naturally as talking. This is communication, which all of us are capable of when we are born. But, as adults, we often forget how to do it. Furthermore, we all communicate with you every day in our dreams. You can call it a dream, intuition, coincidence or something else. Once upon a time, a man met the woman he wanted in a bus stop. His friends said, "What a lucky coincidence!" We disagree and say that it's perfect synchronicity. Let's go on!

What can you get from channeling

Channeling is not a way to learn anything. Channeling can be a way for you to access information, achieve something, and become a better person. Channeling will allow you to gain access to all the information available in the Universe. You feel, see, understand it. One could even say that channeling taught me how to speak French. We would counter this by saying that channeling only enabled you to remember these things. Your spiritual agreements and permissions are the only way to control everything that happens during channeling.

If you are afraid that something "bad", "evil" will happen, you can tell your channeling provider that you do not wish to have that experience. It will take some years for the interest to build up within you. Some will argue that they only want the positive information and things received through channeling. Ok, so it may take a while before they realize that this isn't possible.

Let's now look at the ability to relax and concentrate, as well as deep understanding. Let's think of golden-yellow light which is full of joy, excitement, and affection. Channeling allows you to experience peace, harmony, and a deep inner sense of peace. Matt often recommends to do this before entering the channeling states. It is because you will forget all of your questions once you are there. It is a good idea to have an important question ready, and bring it along with you to the empty spot. Keep it in your heart, not in your head. Feelings are energy. So feel your question and allow the golden light to fill the empty space. We will be there to greet you in this light.

Channeling first attempts are usually only for introduction and to get used the process. It's often quite strange. I don't know whether it was real, a dream, an illusion, or another thing. We can tell that it was real if you believe it. You can continue to explore it by asking: "Is someone interested in reaching me?" Is anyone available to help answer questions or to explain a certain topic?

You can choose to feel joy, happiness, or emptiness. This is okay. To feel happiness, smile, to feel joy, to feel peacefulness, to feel love, to feel peace, and to feel joy, do the same. To feel emptiness, you must empty your self. God knows what feelings your spirit guides will give and what thoughts you'll come up. Don't think about it. Just be. You can feel it, no matter how you feel.

It is not necessary to worry when we know God will always take care of us and protect us. Let it happen. Let everything flow into peacefulness...

Ask questions! Asking questions is a great way to learn and you'll get a lot of information.

A few things

They are very easy. They are simple even though we may not wish to reveal them. Every human is free to choose the beliefs and facts they believe. These beliefs are the first to be revealed when you experience a channeling. They will also mirror you. Many people say that they saw "the devil" or something very terrible. Yes, indeed, you saw devil. But to finally overcome this belief, one must first feel, see, and experience the devil. People may have multiple visions. They then declare that they are psychics. Relax, everything is exactly as it is.

You may be wondering why spiritual beings and entities don't want to communicate. The main reason for this is that the person who would like to contact them holds such beliefs. Chaotic and skittish. "I was approached in the world by a being of clear, pure white light. I asked this being for 1000 euros. The being looked at I and then left. "

The story as told by the being is: "It's me who I am." I feel content, at peace, happiness. I continue running along the tunnel towards human cry. Then I see a tense look that frightens me.

It takes some adaptation to reach out even to a familiar person. Channeling takes some adjustment, like when good friends are on a common wavelength. They will always find something to talk over. It's the same for spiritual entities and beings. Just by observation, you can get to know their state. If you look at them, feel and understand their emotions, then this is a being who radiates light with a loving frequency. The loving feelings will flow naturally without aggression. You will find your relationship with each other more intimate and will adapt. Some entities can be strategic and intelligent, and you should adapt your thinking accordingly. Others are full of joy. You can adjust while still feeling the joy. It is important to lower our vibration in order for us to be able adapt with human energy. If we are to see the story through, it is important to take things seriously. :))

So, it's all very exciting! The channeler can also make contact fail, so it's not surprising that this happens often. Sometimes it fails because the channeler has developed their own ideas about the ideal being and who should be going there. Many people believe that the being is going to save the planet. But, beings who visit to communicate are different. A person might think, "Aha! Someone is coming to touch! Yes, I knew! Soon some evil emperor, no - reptile or no - Hitler, will invade us!"

We are simply watching and laughing.

People form secret circles that allow "big channelers", to tell wonder stories. It's an experience we find so amazing!

Let's get on with the business. We will briefly discuss the colors of the beings.

Highly creative people, gold-educated, highly intelligent, creators and teachers.

Yellow-emotive, active beings that are happy to act and work.

White - Love. Harmony.

Green - an observing, deeply loving feeling against everything that is. Such beings are able to observe the small stream of water through the woods, and then look at it with such profound love. The color of green symbolizes calmness, security, and a sense that one is at home.

Light blue – Very loving beings. It can also be intellectual.

Gray-beings do not think, they have no emotions.

Orange - They're energy beings, they want to accomplish something, they want to improve something and are a bit assertive.

Purple - peace, harmony and flow into eternity. This color is uncommon for beings. They are usually angels involved in Healing.

Black- I don't know the reason, but such colors are often positive. It could be that a dear relative or lover who has died wants to share a message with you but doesn't want it to shock you. Therefore, they keep it hidden or wear black.

Higher vibrations are associated with lighter bodies and stronger light radiation. Even though the body isn't physical, they emit powerful beams of light. An aura color more "physical", on the other hand, is less saturated. It can be more difficult to see. All the colors listed above are only the basics. For example, white and yellow have many shades and combinations. Because they come in a variety of colors, we can communicate with them to see their energy aura and identify the type of being.

An example: A white-gray aura is peaceful and meditative.

Tediousness can be described as grounding in the emotions. Yellow-gold is highly active, enthusiastic, and very creative. They can also wear multiple colors. They are unable to see the physical body of most energy beings. They can be linked to their civilizations using a Telepathic Network, so you can talk to one creature and see that it is surrounded with many entities.

Next, physical beings. They are mostly humanoid or so-called "alien beings". They are lower-level entities interested in improving their environment. Funniest of all is the idea that they have achieved something so they need to aim at a higher position. This is how different types of ideas can arise from these beings about what should and shouldn't be done. When channeling is needed, it should be seen as information that can be used. Channeling should not be viewed as the final truth, but as one point of view.

Some creatures, for example, would believe that a person must eat. While others would think that a person is an absolute light. Different creatures might disagree and say, "I don't get it. What is the point?" Channeling isn't that serious. But channeling can be a great way to discover more about yourself and your own potential perfection.

Feel the energy

To those who have not meditated before, energy can seem like a fantasy. Channeling is a way to make your dreams come true. There are many sensations that may spontaneously appear until energy harmonizes.

However, it's possible for things to be different in some situations. One woman, for instance, has channeled her energy for years. She lives in the countryside and is close to nature. She is so at peace in wild nature that she experiences harmony and peace. To harmonize all this, she wants to live in an urban environment so she can enjoy the "leftovers" peace and feel "madness."

If you have had more extensive contact with a Being, it is possible to feel overwhelmed. Anonymous Someone was an example of someone who channeled a spirit that can create its entire universe, new spaceships, planets and more using only its consciousness. Anonymous Someone realized, upon contacting the being, that the universe is a thought, just energy. After channeling Anonymous Someone, Anonymous Someone felt shocked. The world around his seemed unreal and artificial. Training is required to be able to channel, and also exit, the channeling state. It is important to learn slowly as you do not have the time or resources to rush.

After each channeling you should close any electrifyingly sensitve channeling channels. They can be closed using feelings. Then you can just move on to your daily tasks and stop paying any attention. Sometimes you may feel some discomfort. If this is the case, you can try to pull out this energy by moving it from the top your head down to your feet to your feet. It is also possible to drink lots and walk through the forests, as nature will easily absorb your extra energy.

Next. There are certain beings that can cause an unpleasant reaction, such as nausea, itching and any other strange or inexplicable feeling. These reactions are due to large energy variations with these beings. They will recede after the second and third times.

Communication can often take place in dreams. So before you go to bed, ask questions and receive answers. It's easy to communicate in this way. The spirit guide who "shows the dream" often remains behind-the scenes and only provides the "scenario." This information is mostly for people who are nearly ready to meet their spirits guides.

Many people mistakenly believe that these beings are different from them. It is usually the case that beings who initiate communication, are actually you in another space and time, another life, or possibly another aspect of yourself, which is now coming back to visit. Some people are creative; others are technically proficient. One aspect of them is either in an ideal world, or the contrary, where intelligent thinking can be found. These aspects are able to help you get better and enhance your individual skills.

Channeling for personal development

If you are a channel, it is your consent and wish to channel. You can share information that helps others understand themselves. I should make a small comment: channeling or fortune telling is not a trade. Channeling can be more personal and spiritual. Although channeling may seem like a solution to all of their problems, it is more about helping to understand the root cause, and not just predicting what the future will bring. However, there may be a helper if they are able to assist others. This spirit guide will often help the questioner.

For personal growth, the second option is channeling. You can channel your thoughts, feelings, and visions to help you grow if you work within a particular industry, whether it is creative, intellectual, or otherwise. Nikola Tesla is a scientist, mystic, author of many yet to be explained inventions, and also a physicist. He wanted to know how meditation, dreams and channeling could help him receive visions. This led to a lot of change in the world. It's similar for artists: da Vinci's incredible views of the world, time, and place, as well as Mozart's ability to channel music. He was the composer of the music, and had the ability so effortlessly to create that everyone could experience the same musical world he experienced.

Mozart's remark about people: They didn't feel any, it was a torture for them to be told what to do. Too bad! This is what a human cannot understand!

Anyone can gain the information that will help them to find their personal path. For this type of channeling, however, it is crucial to ensure that the channeler has a clean mind. If the channeler has thoughts that are not helping the process, the channeler will most likely have troubles.

We now have the most basic information about channeling. Now we can get to the nuanced. For instance, if we believe the white light and absolute feeling of Existence to be the highest, then in order to communicate directly with these forms energy, we must disconnect from all thoughts, wishes, and desires. Only then can you call someone to contact who is from Existence's and God's loving presence and absolute light. If you feel this light, it is important to not let your emotions or thoughts cloud the experience.

Relax and let this light align your energetic body. Consider this ongoing alignment, even when you see a person or a peaceful white light.

Keep at it until the peace is felt in the body and the collective energy. You will eventually change and adopt a new way you think. It is easy to then start the communication.

Keep in mind that you are now in an entirely different world. They are very different beings. In order to channel the energy, you both must adapt. This is usually done using a specially prepared interspace. There can be a breakdown of joy and feelings of endless love. They will intensify for as long as there is adaptation of the body to the consciousness.

Let's move on. Ask for help if you're having trouble talking to someone, or experiencing something that isn't what you want. Why is it not working? Why doesn't the communication go through? Ask until you receive answers. Channeling is a process that involves many things. This will prepare you for the future.

Now, the most important.

Why is channeling beneficial for everyone?

It's like a bridge from darkness to light. It enhances your ability to perceive, understand, find truth and have a sense of revelation. It promotes collective and personal consciousness development at higher levels.

A few final tips for those who've had contact with an animal, or who want to clarify some of the following:

How can you tell that it's not your mind who is talking?

It's easy: If you experience an energy-like feeling in your head, if your thinking is different, if your information is from another source, it will be exactly what you feel. Sometimes the information is received with a sense of "freshness" and a seal. It could also include an image. The being may even choose to reveal itself to you. Communication sessions occur telepathically, rather than over the phone. It's important that you get to know it gradually.

Why do you feel I am certain I have this information before?

Yes. It is much easier to access the person's memories. Additionally, if information has been sent before and is appropriate for the case/question in question, it's much easier to retrieve the information from the person. Negative information isn't likely to be spread by beings. They will often enhance it in the same way that people do. If the information you receive is disturbing, negative, or intimidating, it is most likely that it is your mind. If channeling causes doubts, you should remember that doubts, while they can be strong, are just energy. You must harmonize them. Why? It is only information. There's no reason to doubt it.

Doubt can be a fascinating thing by itself. For instance, if we receive new information, we may doubt that it is true. Even if we already know the source of the information, we may still question whether it's our thoughts or a different source. These doubts, however, will vanish with the passage of time and self-confidence.

How can it tell if its a light-being or not?

The majority of beings won't tell you what to do and what to fear. They also won't explain how to call them or who they are. Light beings often ask you "What do want to learn?". They usually only respond to the question, and offer no additional information. You can tell them that it's enough to stop contact. If contact does not cease, then - oops... it's just your mind! You're interfering so please stop!

What, then, is a living being? Although beings have many similarities, their personalities are very different. If you feel "Wow. What an interesting sensation", then you can almost immediately notice that this is not your natural state. This is because it is something outside of you. If you don't have any impressions or feelings that are interesting, it's likely that there is nothing more.

If, for instance, a light-being appears, it is meditative. When we become hyperactive, some of its harmony, peace, and calmness are taken over. The appearance of a hyperactive being causes us to become so active we do not know how stop. An alien entity appears to us, and we believe it to be a robot. It is possible, but not always, for these are just a few scenarios.

There are also beings out there that are friendly and do not disappear. Then you can question why. They may be trying to communicate or show you something.

Remember that there is the Law of Free Will. The universe obeys it.

Don't forget to be confident in who you are! Make sure you know who and what you are. This is normal. Once we recognize it, it can be discarded. It's a way of living with a friend. In time, we learn to assume their character traits.

Be aware of who you are and where you come from. It will also serve as a point-of-reference against which to see what is occurring. By being aware, we can eliminate our old energies.

Feel free to ask questions and share your concerns in our channeling forum.

www.art-of-peace.info

People who know too little go crazy

A short observation made after contact was made with people who read a lot, but have never been in contact other beings or entities. People who have been exposed to books with complicated terminology ("101 reason why you should be careful") can feel trapped. They are not in touch with their inner self. When some light being really begins to communicate, your mind will go crazy and rave because many "self-installed program" will start conflicting and strike out. Such people may experience headaches, blood pressure fluctuations, and stabbing pains in the solar plexus or by their ribs. Because these places are where the inner energetic conflicts can be felt, they often feel the effects of the stress. This is a good lesson. We recommend the golden phrase - It doesn't matter, really it doesn't matter! You don't have anything to worry about as God will always take care you.

So why should anyone be worried?

Permission code

Enrico suggests that you create your own permission code. It says: "I am willing to allow myself to be in this situation or live this life in order that I can only experience positive, harmonious energy exchanges." This is a way to give yourself permission for the type of communication we desire. It also allows us to automatically encode ourselves to experience everything in an harmonious way. It is not that we must communicate only with the angels, ancient teachers, and so forth. We also have other spiritual beings which, when appropriate, can help us to learn many useful lessons. It is important that you understand yourself and how to "program", what you would rather not experience. By expressing it, we can communicate it to the higher peace & light so that all beings, substances, etc., can see and comprehend your free will, and also respect it.

The Fear of Failure

Fear is often viewed as a barrier and obstacle by many people. Here's a story that I tell about a woman who became afraid. She was terrified that the man she was being approached would kill her, as she felt she was being manipulated by someone with a higher vibration. Even amongst friends, she became extremely skittish. Before going to bed she locked her door so that her imaginary killer wouldn't get in and kill. After she fell asleep, she experienced a terrible, cold, unpleasant feeling in her abdominal region. When she felt this feeling, I reminded her of what I had previously told her - to feel it, feel the sensation, and then release it. These words became her mantra. After a while, she felt her entire body become engulfed by a more disgusting feeling. She also felt a coolness flowing from her head. Later she experienced a pleasant feeling. This is just one of many stories.

I was fearful of bad spirits and the possibility that they would either take me away, kill or take my soul, or that God would punish. I also believed that my fears would be realized. These fears made me so anxious that I was unable to sleep. I laid down on the couch and said, "Okay. Let's go. I will go if I need to. I will also go if I must. I am ready to get punished!" My initial reaction was to feel coolness. I don't think so! I thought, "That must have been it, devil has taken my soul!" Then, suddenly, I began to laugh - where did that idea come from? My body began to feel cold and then it vanished completely. It made me giggle so much that I could not even picture it. My solar plexus became relaxed and all my stabbing sensations vanished. I felt like a bright light was shining over me. I heard a voice from an angel. He smiled lovingly and said "I'm your angel." "Great!" - I answered. It was indeed amazing.

One thing that I learned from beings about energies was that we each believe in our own energy. It's often fear or doubt, sadness, and other undesirable energy that enters the body's current energy field. These are low-energy manifestations and are not very noticeable in daily living. However, higher energy causes them to move and you start to feel them. It is an inexplicable, horrible feeling. Sometimes the mind will send it timid thoughts. This energy will persist within us until the day we can get rid. This energy can be found in certain areas of our body, including the abdomen and ribs. This causes this disgusting feeling. People have bad dreams and nightmares often, which can make them feel bad when they wake up in the morning. Your spirit guides will show you these dreams in order to help you feel that you have the energy. After we show this energy, our spirit guides will activate it in us and it will start to feel. This is the right moment to allow this energy to flow through you. Once it has become so active, it will vanish into the sun. Metaphorically, you could compare them with some creatures: tiny fluffy bears with funky emotions. They will awaken when they sense fear or another negative feeling and can then go away. To release these emotions, we must learn to not let them return.

The same applies for emotional issues. It's a setback in our lives to feel the sadness and emotions. It is possible to feel a great sense of affection and love. This symbolises the purification from emotional traumas. Do not rush into channeling. These emotional burdens can sometimes cause shock and severe reactions if they are released too quickly. At the beginning of channeling lessons, it is best to not hurry and take small steps. You should channel 1 minute at first, and then 3 minutes at a time over the course of the week. As fear, anxiety, and other negative emotions slow down, so will the need to hurry. Be deliberate and don't rush, and your mind will ease off. Channeling abilities won't disappear. As there are many emotional and/or physical challenges that need to overcome, we make it more difficult for ourself by hurrying. If you take it slow, there is a possibility that you won't feel it. The background will make it much more quieter, and it will be hard to notice. The intensity of the channeling process can cause you to wake up in the middle of the night.

If you find it difficult to fall asleep and experience nightmares, then close the channels. As you would close any door or image, you can close these channels. This is how we learn to stop energy flowing, and so all of our thoughts can become irrelevant. If our channels are not closed, we can see, feel, and experience all thoughts. While most people have thoughts before bed, it is common for them to think of many things. But, if these thoughts start to become a part of our momentary experience, it can be difficult to fall asleep. This can make it very difficult to fall asleep if there are thoughts of fear, or negative emotions. Let's not waste time, and let's learn small steps. There's nothing you have to prove, to yourself or others. Don't get too attached to the past or dwell on them until you are ready for answers. I remember having a terrible dream. It even gave me shivers. This is why I channeled my thoughts to seek out the truth. A strong feeling of nonexistence activated in me, the chaos of my brain. It felt as though the walls were crumbling and for the next few days, I felt really bad. You should avoid getting into anything that you're not ready for. Also, ask during channeling whether it is really necessary. As you begin to learn, it is important that you don't "sneak about" with the channeling. Ask any channeling expert questions. The replies you receive will be less harsh, but they'll still be as effective.

Another story is one about loneliness. One woman said that she had met her own soulmate in meditation. She was a poor, lonely Indian woman living in great poverty. She began to weep loudly and felt awful when she was asked about her identity. The Indian woman made her feel so sorry she began to cry.

The woman only saw an Indian woman who was alone. However, the solitude energy in her current incarnation activated strongly through these visions. Her eyes lit up and her tears represented that the connection between our lives is restored. She asked me: "Why am I choosing this?" I responded: "Your soul exists in the highest worlds of Existence. The beings from Existence are made aware of a true love through repentance, compassion. It is through emotional trauma that we can discover our true nature, infinite love, and learn from it. The more we experience compassion, the more we will come to appreciate it. You could sense the highest love, compassion and empathy when you were with her.

These examples can be used to help you see and deal with any type of unfavorable energy.

Do you feel uncomfortable?

My personal experience with spirit entities

Enrico was my first, most extraordinary, brightest, most affecting and positively impactful example. It was difficult at first to understand what was really happening. I asked what was going on and they answered that you were starting to telepathically talk with anyone you choose. It seemed very difficult to me. They said that it was part of the awakening process of planet Earth. I thought about it for a while and decided that if my brain can communicate, then I would be able to hear from someone who could tell me something fresh and new. Unexpectedly, Enrico, the being that we now call Enrico, approached me. He was energetic, joyful, and smiled. This is so exciting!

He then ran back to his buddies and began dancing from joy. I watched as he danced and wondered how it was possible. I find his conversations amusing, funny, and he doesn't show any signs of sadness. I didn't feel depressed after that because, as he stated, we can choose our sadness or sorrow! Watch the world rejoice!

Enrico's aura color is yellow-white/golden. I asked him, "Are you one of the highest beings there are?" I replied, "No, not yet. There are many interesting things in the universe that I can experience!"

I started to laugh when I realized that there was no hurry. I can't wait for any experience. It is my choice to be happy and/or to grieve.

I created the Enrico universe's chair in yellow/golden white.

A very specific being from another galaxy

This being was also one aspect of me. It became close to him when I started to have an interest in Cosmos and to think about the theories. It took some time for the alignment to occur with this being. The being was silent but I knew from my previous experiences that the alignment was still happening. It lasted approximately 10 mins. The first answers to the questions came almost instantly - yes and not. After only 30 minutes, they were able to make sentences because this being was beginning to understand me and my mind. They answered my question that they are a highly precise civilization of constructors and builders who travel through space and create a variety of things from natural resources such as stones and temples. I asked him why he was the one who did that. He replied that they are extremely precise and accurate. I asked them what the name of their civilization was.

They have a calm aura, and are not hyperactive like Enrico. The light of white symbolized their ability to fulfill certain Divine tasks. Although they were filled with great sincerity, their efforts were absorbed by the monotony, which left it in balance. I asked them: "Have we ever built any pyramids on Earth?" They replied "No, but other planets have." To my question about why they didn't, they replied that the pyramid emitted a light beam which is aiming at other planets and creating a space map. They act as navigation points in space and are useful for those who travel in astralspace or with spaceships. Because they are very precise, they are able to make maps. They can help other civilizations navigate in space. He showed us our Solar System as a tiny object. However, to us, they travel through Sirius. Ocup is even bigger. Our Solar system and Ocup can be seen as third planets from the Sun when you follow the beam of light. I asked them if the map was ever changing. They stated repeatedly that the map doesn't change and that it is always accurate.

Then, I asked if it is possible to travel by land without needing fuel. He suggested that I use the train. This made me giggle. "But if i would like to travel across the ocean?" He suggested that I use gliders. "There are also maps of winds, which show where the glider might fly independently, and not lose speed. Cyclones and anticyclones lift the glider or bring it to the ground." He also mentioned that birds are able to fly for many years, knowing the winds well, and without using much physical energy.

A being on another planet that didn't like me

Once I was convinced, I set out to find new Space-based beings. I asked my spirit-guides for an alien contact. Then I saw something very odd in front me. Although the alien looked very much like the human, it was rude and frustrated. When I asked it where it was headed, it answered with "SPACE". It also showed me photos of spaceships that can fly. However, the directions were only to the right or straight. It was quite difficult to maneuver them. The incompatibility our energies made the conversation short and painful. He was not interested in speaking because he was angry at either himself or his spaceship. I felt his energy low, so my body had unpleasant anxiety for almost half an hour.

Advanced alien civilizations

My interaction with this civilization was lengthy and fascinating. They wore a black mask and were dressed in black like the Star Wars villain. They ate strange-looking snacks as well as reptiles, but were extremely friendly and peaceful. They also showed how they make spaceships. Space construction is much more stable and durable than traditional methods. He explained how all space is just consciousness. This was scary for me as my human brain wasn't ready to accept that it is only thought and consciousness. Although most of the matter is solid, there is still a thought process and consciousness. This understanding allows them so much advancement, including the ability to fly and to create various enhancements. They also spoke of their nearby civilizations, tiny Sun-like solar-like planets. These are very similar to Enrico's moon! I laughed and they added: "If the Sun is ever covered by something, then we will be able to know that we have reached the Earth." I laughed even more, as the idea was that their ships would cover the Sun to cover large areas of Earth. Although my thoughts were a bit strange for a while, the conversation was very long and I gained a lot positive emotions.

Neutral beings

I asked my spirits guides to locate a neutral entity with which I could talk. The spirit being of a forest appeared to me, and it looked similar to a tree. I began to ask questions. They told me their planet does not revolve around a sun, that they need sunlight, and that they are either closer to the Sun, or near another star, but they are not too close or too far. Their rotation is neutral and not dependent on other stars. Additionally, their planetary systems are made of several stones (or rocks), on which are trees and water. Their planet is composed several rocks that revolve around each other. Special levitating blocks of stone can also be used to jump from one piece of rock to the next. It seemed strange. He said that he was unconscious at the time, and that he would not remember any details. However, he was surprised to discover that he had known this beforehand. I laughed, and said that all people are alike. These beings showed me that there are many planetary systems which travel in space without any dependence on the other.

Child-like beings Plejarians.

These beings have a lot in common with humans. I realized that they were humans in the future or future human civilization. They traveled and lived on other planets, then returned to the people. It was obvious that they possess a faintly visible blue aura. When they feel aggression, they quickly disappear. For them, we seem like savages. However, they act like tiny children. They explained that they fly to Earth because they want to help others. What I admire most about them is their lack of aggression. When they see someone laughing at someone else on the streets, they will cry and want to run. I was chatting with a friend and asked how he could find some income. This being did not reply, but simply pointed to aggression energy. Aggression energy causes us to want what we want. Their definition of aggression is even a "no" word. This impressed me tremendously. It was a great communication.

Consciousness in various forms

They are difficult to explain because they don't exist as beings. It is just nothing, but it's a form of electricity. One of them was known as the observer. This type of energy can keep an eye on events for thousands of years. When I was in touch with this being, I could watch every moment for an entire hour without moving. As a observer, through the centuries, and in eternity, much like a stone standing in the sand, seeing all that is. There's no rush, stress, anything is possible, nothing is reached, nothing is achieved. All that is needed is to observe the world around you. The bicycle passed me in the actual life at that moment. I opened my eye and saw the bicycle moving through my consciousness. It seemed that the bicycle was moving slowly through time. This moment will soon end. This human life can feel like a trifle. But, I am able to keep it in balance, peace, and watch, shaping my perfection.

Higher self

So far I've been in contact with my Higherself three times. But, I now receive information that the experience is different for everyone. I can only briefly describe the experience. My Higher Self sees a golden light. A strong golden energy started to flow from me as I saw a glowing golden light, a golden blossom blooming above my head and it was followed by a strong golden light. I was drawn to it by my inner feelings like I was to the Sun. And after asking the question "Who do you think you are?" I was told that I stood opposite of myself. It was filled with great energy and a lot of joy. Then I received the following information: "I'm you. You are a small piece of me. Your entire existence is in constant communication with me. All my experiences are also yours. It is you who carries my entire life to me so that I can see it. When you start to experience miracles and other coincidences in your daily life, you will find that it is I who speaks to them. This will allow you to understand my nature." I watched a golden light and saw myself in the lotus place. While I radiated a light of happiness and joy, I also realized it was only an image to help me understand.

The other night, I resolved to contact my Higher Self once again. I sat down and spoke my wish. A golden tunnel appeared. The voice said to me, "You are infinitely love, right at this moment," and I was able to hear the words. There was no sense of time. Only an absolute now.

Different story - A woman wrote me that her spirit guides and entities wanted to be communicated with. I said that while I can't promise anything I can guarantee someone will show up. I felt a pancake-like object appear above my head. It was filled with white crystalline light and it filled me up from the top to my heart. The woman explained that they know who they are because of the meditations through which they came to her. The light of white crystalline light continued to shine, so the radiation became more powerful and more bright. I fell more in love with it. The woman called out for light, and it came to my aid. The light started to manifest in the form of the female. It took some time, and it was very powerful.

Another story. While channeling, a friend of mine inquired to the being "Who are you in contact?" My friend did not get the answer. The being revealed him to me. I saw a small, crystal-clear boy who, with a joyful smile, said to me in a clearly audible tone: "Tell his not to worry!" My friend agreed. "You know what, I don't even have to translate it. The boy simply said it in clear Latvian. This was not about money. It's not about any difficult situations. The happy, smiley little boy, who was full of heaven, impressed me. I was not sure if it was a lizard or dog. He also had his little buddy. When a friend saw it, he was excited and felt very happy.

Existence, Beings

This is the best story so far and will be published separately in "Planet Existence". The loving, crystalline woman said that the same being with the luminous, crystal-clear light came to her. He wisely explained about the darkness in people's minds, of consciousness, and that God Himself is an absolute. I thought to me, "Well if possible let's attempt to connect to their." A man with long hair & beard, dressed like an ancient Roman, appeared in my consciousness. He smiled and looked at us. I admired his handsomeness and charm with his confidence. I felt a strong connection and the white light filled every part of my body. I shared with the woman that I was experiencing total euphoria. She replied that it was her! The woman asked what I was doing. This being smiled and replied that he knew it was him. Peace, happiness is what it is. I felt at peace and contentment when this being started to lead me to his world. I felt that I was finally free.

Strong, unconditional, unconditional and unconditional love. This lightens my body and makes me shine. It's almost like experiencing an uncontrollable flow of energy or spiritual orgasm. I saw a sheep eating grass and everything was filled with love. It's hard to explain how every moment was perfect. This being smiled and stood beside me. There was no desire nor incline to achieve anything. They are aware of absolute harmony and bliss, and have reached perfection. They are the souls. They don't have depression or thoughts about the future. It is the ultimate perfection. I was overwhelmed and tearful. It was such an incredible adventure! Why is it that people don't get to this point? Too much thinking. It is because we think too much. Peace and harmony do not come from thinking. They can only be found in a state of mind that does not include thoughts. Harmony and peace are a step towards understanding these beings.

My personal views on channeling

From personal experience, I can confirm that the higher the being the more redundant. Higher beings won't use phrases such "Aaa", Eee and Hmmmm, or mmhhh." Instead, they will use information that has multiple meanings. You should not ask general questions when communicating with these beings. For example, "a Moon" in Latvian can refer to any number of things, such as the moon being Earth's natural satellite or calendar month. In Latvian, the question "what is a moon?" would cause confusion. I suggest that you write down your question, then re-read it to understand why other beings may not understand it, and then adjust accordingly. This is often the reason that the answers don't come.

It is possible to channel a being, who once was a human, and communicate smoothly because that being is familiar in human thinking. People in the audience, if they are channeling publically, tend to loosen up and get more clarity about what they can and cannot do. The future human spoke very freely once I did so, using our facial expressions and gestures. Because this was a man, he could even be flirty with females! This was because the information was packaged and prepared for human comprehension.

www.ingramcontent.com/pod-product-compliance
Lightning Source LLC
Chambersburg PA
CBHW071124130526
44590CB00056B/1777